Business Rule Concepts

Getting to the Point of Knowledge

Second Edition

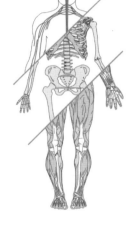

by Ronald G. Ross

Principal, Business Rule Solutions, LLC
Executive Editor, BRCommunity.com
Co-Chair, Business Rules Forum Conference

Spo

Business Rule Concepts
Getting to the Point of Knowledge

Second Edition

by Ronald G. Ross

10 9 8 7 6 5 4 3 2 1

ISBN 0-941049-06-X

To Vanessa

Acknowledgments

I would like to thank Terry Moriarty (Inastrol), Co-Chair of the Business Rules Forum Conference, and Gladys S.W. Lam (Business Rule Solutions, LLC), Executive Director of the Business Rules Forum Conference, for making this second edition of *Business Rule Concepts* possible.

I would also like to thank Keri Anderson Healy, Editor of the *Business Rules Journal*, BRCommunity.com, for her editorial assistance and her many suggestions for clarifying and enhancing the first-edition drafts of the material and then, unbelievably, seven years later going through the whole process yet again for this second edition.

In addition, I would like to thank Marie Yang, Business Director of Business Rule Solutions, LLC, for her assistance in the book's production.

Contents

Introduction

The Business Rule Vision

The Marvelous Organism

The human body is marvelous in many respects, not the least of which is its mechanics. Roughly, support for the mechanics of the human body has three basic components, separate yet intimately interconnected, as follows.

Structure is provided by the bones, which are organized and connected within the skeleton. The skeleton provides both a framework for carrying the weight of the other components as well as a semi-rigid scheme around which the other, softer components can be organized.

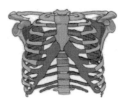

Power is provided through the muscles, which are connected to the bones. The muscles enable motion based on the framework provided by the skeleton. Since motion is what we see happening from outside the body, the muscles seem most directly responsible for the behavior we perceive.

Control is provided by the nervous system, which connects to the muscles. Nerves indirectly connect muscles to other muscles through long series of connections passing through the brain. Responses to all stimuli are coordinated through the firing of nerve impulses — no firing, no movement, and therefore no behavior.

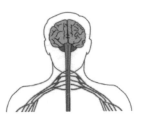

These basic mechanical components are familiar to us all. In a moment, we will see how the mechanics of business systems can be viewed in the very same terms. As we examine the analogy, several observations about the mechanics of the human body are worth keeping in mind.

- All three components are *essential*. The human body literally cannot function without all three.

- The three components are all interconnected — that is, they are *integrated* with each other. For example, tendons connect muscle to bone. Successful behavior depends on this integration.

- Each of the three components is *specialized* for a particular role or responsibility. Each optimizes for its particular task. Mixing or combining the three components would provide a much less effective solution. Also, specialization provides for greater simplicity. Think about how much more complex bones would be if they incorporated muscles or how much more complex muscles would be if they incorporated nerves.

- The nervous system in some sense is the most important component because it provides coordination and control for the other two. The body is certainly capable of behavior without a well-organized nervous system — but not *effective, adaptive* behavior. Literally, you cannot operate at your best with only half a brain!

A New View of Business Systems

I believe that business systems should be organized in a manner similar to the mechanical system of the human body. Let's revisit the three components of that system, thinking now about the business (or some business capacity within it[1]) in place of the human body.

Structure

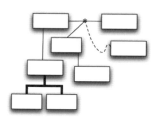

Structure is provided by organized — that is, *structured* — knowledge about the most basic things we can know about the business. These 'basic things we can know' are often simply taken for granted — just like the human skeleton in everyday activity. They consist of core *concepts* of the business and the basic, everyday logical or factual *connections* we make between concepts.

Introduction

Think of these core concepts as bones and the connections as ligaments (that is, bone-to-bone connections).

- Just as each bone has a particular shape that is optimal for its purpose and location, so too must each core concept have a carefully-crafted 'shape.' A concept's shape is given by its definition, which must be clear, concise, and well suited for its business purpose.

- Every bone or concept must also have a standard name. In the business rule approach, the standard names for concepts are called *terms*.

- Each ligament also has a particular shape that is optimal for its purpose and location. Similarly, each logical or factual connection between concepts must have a standard 'shape.' In the business rule approach, these connections are called *facts*. Their standard shapes are given by special wordings that reference the appropriate terms.

A drawing or diagram of the complete human skeleton helps us understand how all the bones fit together. To illustrate the overall structure of terms and facts, it is likewise helpful to create a drawing or diagram. Our name[2] for such a diagram is *fact model*.

A fact model provides a framework, in many ways like a skeleton, in two basic respects.

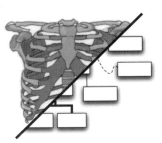

1. A fact model literally provides a standard scheme around which the other components can be organized — that is, the 'basic things we can know' *in common* throughout the business.

2. A fact model carries the 'weight' of the organization — that is, its *collective* or *shared know-how*.

Power

Power is provided by *processes*, which operate on the terms and facts. Whereas the fact model provides for structure, the processes provide for activity.

When we think about a business system, the processes are often the first things that come to mind. They represent the most visible aspect of the business system because they literally *do* what the business needs to get done (for example, take the customer's order). However, viewing a business system as merely a collection of processes makes no more sense than viewing the human body as merely a collection of muscles. Any organism is much more than that — whether human or business.

Control

Control is provided by *rules*, which constrain processes (the 'muscles') to act only in certain ways deemed best for the business as a whole. In the human body, there are literally hundreds of muscles, which must act in concert. If they do not, the resulting behavior at best will be less than optimal. At worst, serious damage can result (for example, hyperextension of a limb) that will significantly reduce the body's overall capacity to act.

Similarly, business systems literally consist of hundreds (or thousands) of 'muscles' (processes), which must act in concert. If they do not, the business will also behave in a less than optimal fashion. In some cases, serious damage can result (for example, loss of customers, squandering of resources or opportunities, and so on) that will significantly reduce the business's overall capacity to act (that is, its competitiveness and/or effectiveness).

In the human body, we take many control actions of the nervous system for granted. For example, who thinks about the impulses sent to the heart to make it beat — unless, of course, something goes wrong? Or who in the process of saying, "Ouch!" thinks much about the jerk reflex that causes the hand to move so quickly off the hot stove? As long as all runs smoothly, we can apply our mental faculties to a higher purpose — whether for working, solving problems, or simply planning a fun lunchtime getaway.

Introduction

Similarly, while things run smoothly in the business, we can take the control actions of the rules for granted and concentrate on matters requiring a higher order of intelligence. Until a rule 'breaks' somehow — and that is a very important possibility, of course — we can focus on the more creative aspects of business operation and strategy.

Summary

A business is very much like a human body — a living organism. Let's revisit the observations I made earlier about the mechanics of the human body, now applying them to business systems.

- All three components — structure (terms and facts), processes, and rules — are *essential*. A business literally falls apart — disintegrates — without all three.

- The three components are obviously interrelated. For example, the processes act on knowledge about things represented in the fact model. These actions, in turn, are subject to the rules. Successful business behavior depends on effective *integration*. These fundamental interrelationships must obviously be taken into account.

- Each of the three components is *specialized* for a particular role or responsibility and optimized for its particular task. Mixing or combining them would provide a less effective solution. The business rule approach therefore recognizes the importance of factoring out the rules. We call this *Rule Independence*[3]. As a fringe benefit comes a huge simplification in the processes (the 'muscles' of the business system). In the business rule approach it is legitimate for the first time to talk of truly *thin* processes — a long-standing goal among many information technology (IT) professionals.

- In many ways rules are the most important component since they provide control for the other two. The business and its systems are certainly capable of behavior without a well-organized set of rules — but not *effective, adaptive* behavior. Literally, rules are what make a business more than half-smart in how it operates.

The second point above emphasizes that the three basic components of business systems must interrelate in an integrated fashion. Just how they do that represents the new vision of business systems at the heart of the business rule approach. As this book explains, the implications of this new vision are far-reaching.

About this Book

This book is divided into two main parts, as follows.

Part 1: Key Concepts of the Business Rule Approach

Part 1 is aimed toward the general reader seeking to understand the basic ideas of the business rule approach. In the human body, each of the individual components of the mechanical system described above has its own inner workings. In fact, there are individual sciences focusing almost exclusively on each particular component. Each of the basic components in the business rule approach must also be understood individually. Each too has its own particular 'physiology.'

- Chapter 1 examines structure (terms and facts), as embodied in the core concepts of the business and their logical connections. In particular, this chapter explains fact models and what they represent.

- Chapter 2 examines guidance and control, as embodied in rules. This chapter provides exciting new insights about the inner workings of rules.

- Chapter 3 discusses some of the implications of the business rule approach for business — that is, *getting to the point of knowledge.*

Part 2: Concepts of the Business Rule Approach for the Practitioner

Part 2 is aimed toward the practitioner seeking more complete understanding of each 'physiology.'

- Chapter 4 examines structure (terms and facts) more fully.

- Chapter 5 examines rules more fully.

- Chapter 6 examines power, as embodied in processes. The business rule approach offers a new view of processes, one that is radical in its simplicity. Ironically, it is in that very simplicity that the big picture of business systems emerges in the business rule approach.

Notes

1 By *business capacity* I mean some significant subset of the business, possibly encompassing one or more business processes, functional areas, and/or decision points. To simplify matters, from this point forward in the discussion I will drop the additional *or some business capacity within it* whenever *business* appears and assume you understand I also mean any significant subset of the business.

2 *Our* (and 'we' as used later) refers to Business Rule Solutions, LLC (BRS). *Name* refers to the name that BRS uses in Proteus[R], the BRS methodology for business engineering and business rule capture and analysis.

3 Refer to the *Business Rules Manifesto* by the Business Rules Group, published as an Appendix to this book.

Part 1

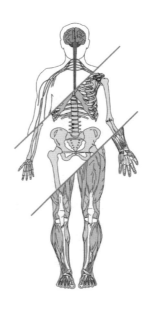

The Key Concepts of the Business Rule Approach

Chapter 1

What You Need to Know About Terms and Facts

In the human body, structure is provided by the skeleton. The skeleton has two basic components: the bones and the ligaments that connect the bones. Even though the bones are larger and in a sense more basic, both components are essential.

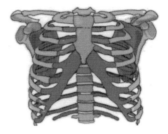

A business system must have a corresponding structure. In the business rule approach, this structure is visualized by means of a fact model, representing the basic skeleton for the knowledge structure of the business. Without any exaggeration, a good fact model is no less important to a business system than a strong and complete skeleton is to the human body.

As in the skeleton for the human body, a fact model likewise has two basic components: terms and facts. These are equivalent to the bones and ligaments, respectively, in the human body. These terms and facts structure basic business knowledge — that is, they represent things in the business that it is possible to know about.[1]

> Terms and facts structure basic business knowledge.

About Terms and Concepts

A *term* is a basic word or word phrase in English or another natural language[2] that workers recognize and use in business communications of all kinds — for example, in agreements, procedure manuals, schedules, directives, instructions, and so on. Requirements for IT systems, and the documentation and help or guidance messages in operational IT systems, are additional forms of business communication.

A term carries a particular meaning for the business, which should be unambiguous given a particular context of usage.[3] Terms are always nouns or qualified nouns. Here are some examples.

customer	employee name	date
prospect	delivery date due	high-risk customer
shipment	manager	employee
order	gender	line item
invoice	status	quantity back-ordered

Our meaning of *term* comes straight from *Webster's*. Note the key words "precisely limited meaning" in this definition.

Term: *a word or expression that has a precisely limited meaning in some uses or is peculiar to a science, art, profession, trade, or special subject*

Merriam-Webster's Unabridged Dictionary, 2000

It is important to note that the particular word or phrase selected as a term represents merely the tip of the iceberg with respect to meaning. More fundamental is the business *concept* for which the word or phrase stands. This concept *must* be defined. That is, the concept a term represents should never be taken for granted. As one practitioner put it, "The more self-evident the meaning of a term is, the more trouble you can expect." As an example, another practitioner from a medium-sized company rattled off six

different (and conflicting!) definitions of "customer" from different parts of his organization.

In the business rule approach, a precise definition for each term must be given explicitly in business-oriented (that is, non-technical[4]) fashion. All facts (and rules) that reference the term will depend on this meaning. Here is an example of a definition, again from Webster's.

Customer: *one that purchases some commodity or service; especially, one that purchases systematically or frequently*

To be included in a fact model, a term should satisfy all three of the following fundamental tests.

Basic: Terms in the fact model represent the most basic things of the business — that is, terms that cannot be derived or computed from any other terms.[5] Any term that can be derived or computed should be expressed as the subject of a rule.

Atomic: Terms in the fact model should represent things that are indivisible — that is, *unitary* — at least as seen from the business's point of view. Terms that have a collective or *composite* sense (for example, *merchandise, personnel, inventory,* and so on) should be broken down into their atomic constituents before being represented in the fact model.

Knowable: Terms in the fact model should always represent things we can know something about, rather than things happening. In other words, a fact model is about *knowledge*, not about the actions, processes, or procedures that produce or use that knowledge. A fact model, for example, might show the terms *customer* and *order*, but it would not show the action *take customer order*.

In the business rule approach, the collection of all terms and definitions is called a *Concepts Catalog*.[6] In one sense, this label is merely a dressed-up name for a glossary. Because definitions are so crucial to organizing large sets of rules, however, this glossary needs to be automated. Such automated support permits changes in the terms to be coordinated directly with all the rules where they appear.

> Every term requires a definition, and
> every definition belongs in the Concepts Catalog.

Using the Concepts Catalog is the way to avoid a "Tower of Business Babel" when building complex business systems. Here then is a fundamental (and obvious) principle of the business rule approach: We will inevitably work more effectively if we all speak the same language!

> A fact model establishes common business vocabulary.

Developing the Business Vocabulary

The core terms of a fact model represent types or *classes* of things in the business, rather than *instances* of those things. For example, a business might have 10,000 customers, but they are represented by the single term *customer*. Incidentally, since the term refers to the class rather than to instances, the term's singular form is preferred for the fact model (that is, *customer* rather than *customers*).

Rules associated with business processes typically address classes rather than instances. Rules about the company's product/services — its special 'know how' — often, however, address instances as well.

- An organization that inspects ships has thousands of rules that reference hundreds of individual parts of a ship.

- A health insurance company has thousands of rules that reference hundreds of individual health care treatments.

Establishing a consistent, 're-usable' business vocabulary covering both classes and pre-defined instances is an important up-front cost of doing business the business-rule way. This activity requires a measure of vision and patience. The business benefits, however, are substantial. Managing, operating, and interacting based on agreed vocabulary is basic not only to improving business communication, but to retaining and/or automating core business 'know how' as well. These are hardly luxuries in a world where staffs are ever more volatile, self-service is rapidly becoming the norm, and delivery platforms are forever evolving.

About Facts and Fact Types

In general, *facts* relate terms, much as ligaments connect bones in the human skeleton.[7] Facts are expressed using structural forms — *sentence forms* — that permit statements of predictable types, especially for rules, to be made about the business. Examples are given in the table. Note that in each example, a verb or verb phrase (italicized below) connects relevant terms. Such factual sentence forms, representing *fact types*,[8] are central to fact modeling.

Factual Sentence Form (Fact Type)	Sample Statement (Rule)
customer *places* order	A customer always *places* at least one order.
shipment *is approved by* employee	A shipment must *be approved by* at least two employees.
shipment *includes* order	A shipment must not *include* more than 10 orders.

Several observations are worth making.

1. Facts types are based on common or shared verbs and verb phrases of the business.[9] In other words, a fact model extends the common business vocabulary in important ways.

> **A fact model extends the common business vocabulary.**

2. Every fact type follows a strict subject-verb-object structure — for example, *customer places order*.[10] This *structuring* provides a way to communicate consistently about how the business concepts logically connect to each other, and provides a foundation for capturing other kinds of knowledge, especially rules.

> **Fact types structure the logical connections we want made between concepts.**

3. 'Terms and facts' is a handy, informal designation used in a business rule approach to refer to the entire collection of concepts, definitions, terms, and fact types that provide knowledge structure for the business.[11] A more accurate designation is *structured business vocabulary*.

> **A fact model represents a structured business vocabulary.**

4. The sentence forms merely establish the fact types; they place no constraints on instances of these facts. For example, *customer places order* represents a fact type. It is inappropriate to state the following as a fact type: *A customer always places at least one order*. This latter statement is more than a fact type — it places a *constraint* on instances of the fact type. Thus this statement is a rule — part of the control aspect of the business system, *not* part of the structural aspect. A rule represents the nerves, not the skeleton!

> Fact types recognize what it is possible to know,
> but given that, no other constraints.

5. Note how the fact types are expressed using verbs (for example, *places*). It is important to remember that these verbs do not represent or label any action, process, or procedure per se (for example, *place order*). Any such operation represents a different aspect of the business system — the power or "muscle" aspect. Think of the fact model as providing the most appropriate way[12] to organize knowledge about the *results* (or potential results) of such operations. In other words, the fact model organizes what we can know as the result of actions, processes, and procedures taking place in the business.

> Fact models organize knowledge about the results of
> operations, not about how these operations actually take place.

Certain important kinds of fact types come in pre-defined 'shapes' that reflect specific kinds of logical connections people make in the business day-in and day-out. As discussed in Chapter 4, these 'shapes' take the form of pre-defined factual sentence forms called *factual connection templates*. There are a half-dozen or so of these, two of which are illustrated briefly below. The kinds of statements that can be made with these templates are increasingly powerful.

Kind of Factual Connection	Factual Sentence Form (Fact Type)	Sample Statement (Rule)
Property	order *has* date taken order *has* date promised	An order's date promised must be at least 24 hours after the order's date taken.
Category	'corporate customer' *is category of* 'customer' 'rush shipment' *is category of* 'shipment'	A rush shipment may include only orders placed by a corporate customer.

The collection of all fact types developed by business people establishes the full and complete scope of the business system in a very important sense. Even if a worker or some automated process produces or expresses facts of some other type(s), we will literally have no way to share such knowledge in a standard and consistent fashion unless the appropriate fact types have been included in the fact model.

> A fact model establishes the basis for shared operational business knowledge.

Using Graphic Fact Models

You might have noticed that even though fact models are usually rendered graphically, no diagrammatic examples have yet been presented. This is not because diagrams are not useful. Just the opposite is true; they are *very* useful. Rather, I wanted to emphasize that a fact model is first and foremost about what we can *know*, or perhaps more importantly, how we can *communicate* about what we can know.

We might call definitions and sentence forms 'word work' or even *wordsmithing*. It is certainly true that such 'word work' can be facilitated by specialists[13] who help clarify and express the thoughts in plain-but-concise business language. But again, the bottom line is business communication. Knowledgeable workers on the business side must originate and understand the definitions and sentence forms. That sometimes proves difficult — not because English is hard, but because expressing what we know about the business in an understandable, agreed-to form can be hard!

> "What we can know" about the operational business and/or its know-how can always be expressed on the basis of natural-language sentence forms.

Getting all the terms and sentence forms to fit together as if in some large jigsaw puzzle can also be a challenge. This is where the graphic fact model diagram plays an important role.

When creating a blueprint for remodeling your house, you can quickly see when the pieces are not fitting together. The eye often spots the problems quite easily. A fact model serves a similar purpose. In doing 'word work' for a large, complex business area, it is often hard to spot the redundancies and overlap. Representing the words and sentence forms graphically makes this easier. Just remember, sponsors and/or the business people should sign off on the terms, definitions, and sentence forms — *not* on graphic fact models.[14]

> The principal deliverable of the fact-modeling part of a business rule project is a set of definitions and sentence forms.

Figure 1–1 presents a simple fact model in graphic form. The fact types for this fact model are listed below it. This list includes several fact types that are *implicit* in the graphic fact model (that is, not labeled explicitly) — these are based on the factual connection templates mentioned earlier. See Chapter 4 for additional discussion.

> A fact model is a blueprint for basic business knowledge.

Figure 1–1. Sample Fact Model for a Library

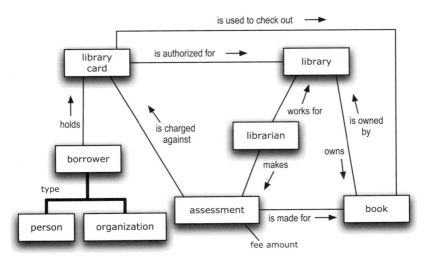

Fact Types for Figure 1–1

Explicit:

- library card *is used to check out* book
- library card *is authorized for* library
- library *owns* book (book *is owned by* library)
- librarian *works for* library
- librarian *makes* assessment
- assessment *is made for* book
- assessment *is charged against* library card
- borrower *holds* library card

Implicit:

- person *is category of* borrower
- organization *is category of* borrower
- assessment *has* fee amount

Summary

A good fact modeler seeks to ensure that each core element of business knowledge (i.e., term or fact type) is represented in the fact model one and only one time and that it does not overlap any other core element. In other words, the fact model ensures that the core elements of business knowledge are *unified* and *unique*. Later, this will provide a way to ensure that all rules are defined consistently and that different actions will operate in consistent fashion.

> By helping to ensure unification and uniqueness of business knowledge, the fact model ensures consistency in business behavior.

Like the skeleton in the human body, the terms and facts in a fact model must represent the *minimum* set needed to provide a suitable framework for the other components. There are no extra bones in the human body —

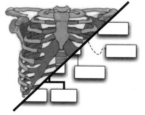 every one has its specific purpose. Adding a bone here or there is not going to improve the body's mechanics. Anyway, bones are relatively expensive because, although essential, they represent overhead to the end result actually desired — namely, *behavior*.

Similarly, a few extra terms and fact types here or there in the fact model will not help the business body operate. And they will prove expensive. A fact model helps ensure there are no extra elements in the basic knowledge of the business.

> A fact model should represent the minimum set of core-knowledge elements.

Some IT professionals believe that if they can get the behavior right, the structure will simply fall into place. That is not our experience at all. It's the body as a whole that matters. You can design a lot of very elegant appendages and a lot of fancy behaviors, but there had better be a well-considered skeleton to hold them all together!

Notes

1   Workers and managers, of course, can know many things about the basic operations of the business. Terms and facts establish which of all those basic things the workers will *share*.

2   For convenience, I will drop the phrase *or another natural language* in the discussion from this point on, with the implicit understanding that the discussion applies to any language, not just to English.

3   From this point forward in the discussion, I will drop *context of usage* when discussing the meaning of terms, with the implicit understanding that this qualification is nonetheless a highly significant one.

4   I mean *technical* here in the sense of IT, not in terms of the products or services of the business. The definition of some terms can be highly technical in a business sense.

5   Such things are sometimes described as *primitives*.

6   This is the term has been used by the Business Rules Group (*http://www. BusinessRulesGroup.org*) since the late 1990s.

7   It is possible for a fact to concern only a single term (e.g., that a person smokes), but this is a relatively minor point for an initial understanding of fact models.

8   *Factual sentence form* is to *fact type* as *term* is to *concept* — that is, a factual sentence form is a *representation* of a fact type.

9   Since this discussion is informal, I will use the designation *fact type* instead of the more correct *expression of fact type* in the discussion that follows. The distinction is that the same fact type can be given by expressions in different languages (e.g., French, Mandarin, and so on), and/or by different sentence forms in the *same* language (e.g., *customer places order*, *order is placed by customer*). In other words, there can be many different *expressions* for the same given *fact type*.

10 A significant majority of fact types of interest for fact models involve exactly two terms; however, fact types involving more than two terms are sometimes appropriate (e.g., person visits city on date). In formal logic, all such sentence forms represent *predicates*.

11 More important than terms are the concepts and definitions they stand for. In addition, most connections of interest between the concepts are fact *types*, rather than *facts* in the formal sense. Nonetheless, "terms and facts" (as in "terms, facts, and rules") is memorable and widely used. It is basic to the <u>business rule mantra</u>, "Rules are based on facts, and facts are based on terms," which dates to the early 1990s work of the Business Rules Group. So I will continue to use terms and facts from time to time in the remainder of this discussion, including in the chapters to come.

[12] To be precise, the *most appropriate way* means anomaly-free and semantically clear. These are criteria that can actually be tested. In relational theory, normalization prescribes tests (the normal forms) for this purpose. Refer to Chapter 11 in Date [2000].

[13] Such as business analysts, fact modelers, terminologists, etc.

[14] Unfortunately, this is more or less the reverse of many development methodologies for IT systems.

Chapter 2

What You Need to Know about Rules

In the human body, control is provided by the nervous system, an organized collection of nerves that connect to the muscles. Responses to all stimuli are coordinated through the firing of nerve impulses — no firing, no movement, and therefore no behavior.

A business system must have similar coordination of behavior. In the business rule approach, this control — better viewed in general as *guidance* — is provided by rules.

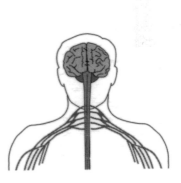

Rules for Guidance

Rules are familiar to all of us in real life. We play games by rules, we live under a legal system based on a set of rules, we set rules for our children, and so on.

Yet the idea of rules in business systems is ironically foreign to many people. Say "rules" and many IT professionals, for example, think vaguely of expert systems or artificial intelligence — approaches deemed appropriate for only very specialized and/or very advanced kinds of problems. Recognition has only come slowly about how central rules actually are to the basic, day-to-day operations of the business.

Not coincidentally, many business-side workers and managers have become so well indoctrinated in *procedural* views for developing requirements that thinking in terms of rules might initially seem foreign and perhaps abstract. Virtually every methodology has been deficient in this regard, whether for business process reengineering, system development, or software design. This is unfortunate for at least two important reasons.

1. Thinking about the control aspect of any organized activity in terms of rules is actually very natural. For example, imagine trying to explain almost any game you can think of — chess, checkers, baseball, football, tennis, and so on — without explaining the rules on which the moves in the game are based. Even if it were possible (that's

doubtful!), explaining things that way would certainly not be very *effective*.

2. Business-side workers and managers have the knowledge it takes to create good rules. What *they* know makes all the difference in the world in playing the business game.

The business rule approach not only depends on good rules but also offers new insights into what they are about, as to be discussed later (in Chapters 5 and 6). Without any exaggeration, good rules are no less important to a business system than a robust, finely-tuned nervous system is to the human body.

The first step in understanding the central role of rules in the business rule approach is simply to relate them to the issue of guidance. The special box opposite presents a light sampling of typical rules,[1] each categorized informally according to the kind of guidance it provides. Note how far-ranging these categories really are. *Every* aspect of operational guidance in a business — or an information/knowledge system that supports it — can be addressed by rules.

The second step in understanding rules — a crucial one — is to understand how they relate to terms and facts (i.e., to a structured business vocabulary[2]). In the business rule approach, rules build directly on terms and facts. Basically, a rule should simply add the sense of *must* or *must not* to terms and facts that have already been defined in the fact model and Concepts Catalog. This is a key feature of business-oriented languages for expressing rules, such as *RuleSpeak*®.[3]

In business problems involving hundreds or thousands of rules — not at all uncommon — there is no way to achieve consistency across such large numbers of rules without a common base of terms and facts. This important principle of the business rule approach was discussed in Chapter 1. That infrastructure of terms and facts is indispensable for *scaling up*.

> Scaling up requires that rules build directly on shared terms and facts.

The third step in understanding rules — also a crucial one — is to understand how rules relate to events. It is to that perhaps non-intuitive subject that we now turn.

Restriction
A customer must not place more than three
rush orders charged to its credit account.

Guideline
A customer with preferred status should have
its orders filled immediately.

Computation
A customer's annual order volume must be computed as total
sales closed during the company's fiscal year.

Inference
A customer must be considered preferred if the
customer places more than five orders over $1,000.

Timing
An order must be assigned to an expeditor if
shipped but not invoiced within 72 hours.

Trigger
"Send-advance-notice" must be performed for an order when the
order is shipped.

Rules and Events

Business systems have addressed the
validation and editing of data since the
first computer programs for business were
written many years ago. Unfortunately,
the programming view of editing and
validating data is a very procedural one,
simply because traditional computer
programs worked that way. With respect
to rules, however, the procedural view
is a very limiting one. It definitely
represents a case of "can't see the forest for the trees."

Rules in the business rule approach are always perceived and expressed
declaratively, independent of processes and procedures. Appreciating the
importance of this principle is key. It inevitably moves us away from seeing
requirements for business systems as essentially a programming problem
and toward viewing them as a true *business* problem. Happily, this view is
also greatly simplifying. Suddenly, the forest emerges from the trees.

Understanding this fundamental principle of the business rule approach requires careful examination of the relationship between rules and events. Intuitively, we know that certain rules apply when certain events occur. But what exactly is the connection between rules and events?

First, it is important simply to recognize that rules and events are not the same. This might seem obvious, but it is nonetheless a common source of confusion.

> **Rules and events are not the same.**

To understand this, we must probe into events more deeply. What is an event? There are at least two ways of looking at events, both correct from their own perspective.

1. **The business perspective**: For the business, an event is something that happens requiring the business to respond, even if only in a trivial way. (Usually, the response is *not* trivial.) For example, a customer places an order. This is an event that requires a well-organized response. Often we try to organize our response to such business events in advance — for example, within business process models, workflow models, procedures, and so on.

2. **The IT perspective:** For an information/knowledge system that supports the business, an event is something that happens and needs to be noted or recorded[4] because knowing about the event is potentially important to other activities, either those occurring during the same time frame or those that might happen later. In the business rule approach, of course, such recording is always based on predefined

terms and facts — that is, primarily on the basis of the fact model. An information/knowledge system can support the fact model in several ways (for example, as a database design, a class diagram, and so on). To simplify matters, let's just say there is some data somewhere in the system that must be updated (created, modified, or deleted) to record the event. Otherwise, the business cannot know about the event.[5] For convenience, I will call these *update events*.

Now, how do events connect with rules? Consider the business rule: *A customer must be assigned to an agent if the customer has placed an order.* Figure 2–1 shows the relevant terms and facts for this rule.

Figure 2–1. Terms and Facts for the Customer Rule

The rule itself has been expressed in declarative manner. This means, in part, that it does not indicate any particular process, procedure, or other means to enforce or apply it. It is simply a rule — nothing more, and nothing less.

Declarative also means that the rule makes no reference to any business event or update event where it potentially could be violated and/or needs to be tested — that is, where it needs to *fire*.[6] The rule does not say, for example, "*When* a customer places an order, then...."

This observation is extremely important for the following reason. "*When* a customer places an order" *is not the only event when the rule could potentially be violated.* Actually, there is another event when this rule could be violated. In business terms this other event might be "*When* an agent leaves our company...." The corresponding update event might be "*When* an agent is deleted...."[7] This other event could pose a violation of the rule under the following circumstances: (a) The agent is assigned to a customer, and (b) that customer has placed at least one order.

In other words, the rule could potentially be violated during *two* quite distinct kinds of events. The first — "*When* a customer places an order ..." — is rather obvious. The second — "*When* an agent leaves the company ..." — might be much less so. Both events are nonetheless important because either could produce a violation of the rule.

This example is not atypical or unusual in any way.[8] In fact, it is quite commonplace. In general, *every* business rule (in proper declarative form) produces[9] two or more kinds of events where it could potentially be violated and/or needs to be evaluated (i.e., needs to fire), both at the business perspective and the system perspective.[10]

> Every rule produces two or more events where it needs to fire.

About Violations of Rules

Let's examine rules that can be violated more closely.[11] What happens when an event occurs that might violate some particular rule?

1. No matter which event it is, at that point the rule should *fire* so that the prescribed test or constraint can be applied.

2. If a violation has indeed occurred, appropriate intervention should ensue.

3. Assuming the end user (that is, the business worker) is authorized and knowledgeable, some explanation should be provided to explain what triggered the intervention. Let's call that explanation a *guidance message* (rather than, say, *error* message), because the real intent is to inform and to shape appropriate business behavior, rather than to reprimand or simply inhibit.

What should the guidance message returned to the business worker say? *The guidance message should contain exactly the same text as was originally given for the rule.* In the example above, this means it should literally read: *A customer must be assigned to an agent if the customer has placed an order.*[12] To put this more strongly, in the business rule approach the rule statement *is* the guidance message.[13]

> The business rule is the guidance message.

In summary, what does this analysis reveal about the relationship between rules and events? First, it illustrates the basic point that rules and events, while related, are not the same. Second, it illustrates that there are always potentially multiple events where any given rule needs to fire. Figures 2–2 and 2–3 provide additional examples to reinforce this crucial point. In the business rule approach, rules are central — *not* events.

> In the business rule approach, rules — not events — are central.

Chapter 2

Figure 2–2. Multiple Events for a Simple Rule

Rule: *A customer must have an address.*

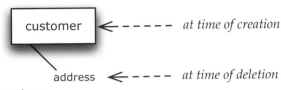

This rule produces...
  Update event #1:   When an instance of customer is created
  Update event #2:   When an attempt occurs to delete (nullify) the value of address

Figure 2–3. Multiple Events for a More Complex Rule

Rule: *A territory must not include more than one of the following:*
        * Non-candidate traditional gas station.
        * Ultra-service.
        * Food outlet.

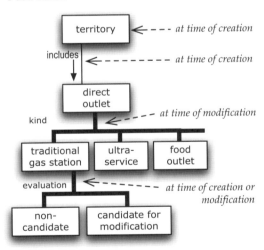

This rule produces...
  Update event #1:   When an instance of territory is created
  Update event #2:   When an instance of direct outlet is added to (included in) an existing territory
  Update event #3:   When an instance of direct outlet already included in a territory changes kind
  Update event #4:   When an instance of traditional gas station already included in a territory gets or changes evaluation

What are the implications? From the business perspective, discovering and analyzing events with respect to rules often proves to be a useful activity in validating rules. Important and sometimes surprising guidance issues (a.k.a. business policy questions) often crop up. As discussed in the next chapters, this technique is one of many for validation and verification of business rules that specialized tools for *business workers* should support.

> Automated support for identifying and analyzing events for rules from the business perspective is an important capability.

On the technical side, discovering and supporting update events becomes a crucial implementation concern, since business systems typically have significant numbers of rules that potentially can be violated *by people*.[14] This can prove an important consideration in acquiring and applying rule engine technologies.

Decision Points

Another target-rich area for the business rule approach is decision points. A decision point is where some critical decision (usually a complex one) must be made. Such a decision typically might have to do with one of

the following kinds of task: configuration, allocation, assignment, classification, assessment, compliance, diagnosis, and so on.

The rules governing such decisions (sometimes called *decision logic*) are often peculiar to and characteristic of the company's *product/service* offerings (a.k.a., *know-how*). These offerings invariably involve the company's special area(s) of expertise.

Examples of such decisions include whether or not to:

- Approve an application for automobile insurance
- Pay a claim
- Buy a stock
- Declare an emergency
- Accept a reservation
- Indicate possible fraud
- Give an on-the-spot discount to a customer
- Assign a particular resource to a given request
- Select a health care service for a patient
- Certify a ship for safety

Such decision points, all rule-intensive, are of vital importance to the business. Capturing the (often numerous) rules in declarative form and organizing them into manageable rule sets should be a key component of every company's IT approach. Unfortunately, most approaches fail to do that — a serious omission.

Is it possible to define all relevant rules well enough for automated decision making to be effective? There are, of course, some very difficult problems (for example, *accurate* weather forecasting) that are beyond the current state of the art. In the typical business, however, a large number of crucial everyday decision points come nowhere near being that complex. The proven answer is *yes*.[15]

So just about every company has two crucial kinds of rules:

- Rules for their product/service *know-how*. These rules are often of the decision-making or inference variety.

- Rules for their business processes. These rules are often of the kind that people can potentially violate.

Examples of these two kinds of rules for three different organizations are given below.

Internal Revenue Service (IRS)

Business Process Rule
- *A processed tax return must indicate the IRS Center that reviewed it.*

Product/Service Rule
- *Calculated total income must be computed as tax return wages (line 1) plus tax return taxable-interest (line 2) plus tax return unemployment compensation (line 3).*

Ministry of Health

Business Process Rules
- *A claim must be assigned to an examiner if fraud is suspected.*
- *An on-site audit must be conducted for a service provider at least once every five years.*

Product/Service Rules
- *A claim involving comprehensive visits or consultations by the same physician for the same patient must not be paid more than once within 180 days.*
- *A claim that requests payment for a service event that is a provision of health service type 'consultation' may be paid only if the service event results from a referral received from another service provider.*

Ship Inspection Agency

Business Process Rules
- *A ship inspection work order must include at least one attendance date.*
- *A ship must involve a client who is financially responsible for inspections.*
- *An inspection due for a ship must be considered suspended if the ship is laid-up.*

Product/Service Rules
- *A ship area subject to corrosion must be inspected annually.*
- *A salt water ballast tank must be inspected empty if the ship is more than five years old.*
- *A barge must have an approved bilge system to pump from and drain all below-deck machinery spaces.*

A Central Role for Rules

The emphasis on rules and their separation from events and processes opens many new doors of opportunity for both IT and the business. Among these opportunities are the following.

Simple consistency: The two or more events where a rule needs to fire are likely to be embedded in at least two and possibly many different processes or procedures.[16] Yet for all of these, there is only a *single* rule. That same rule should fire when any of the events occur in any of the processes or procedures where the rule might be violated and/or needs to be evaluated. By this means, the business rule approach ensures complete consistency in the 'editing criteria' and/ or decision logic applied across all the processes. Especially in the case of rules that can be violated by people, it also ensures there are no holes arising from omissions for less-than-obvious kinds of event.

Adaptability: Separating the rule from the events and processes where it needs to fire allows the rule itself to be specified *in one place*. One-place specification (single-sourcing) means the rule will be easier to find — and to change quickly — once the business system is implemented.[17]

Reengineering: Business processes and procedures are generally organized as responses to business events. Declarative rules, however, are specified in *eventless* fashion. They are the pure essence of the business — a *rulebook* for the business game. For reengineering business processes, this clarity enables better balance between action and guidance, as well as far better results for both individually.

> Rules are essential for effective reengineering
> of business processes.

Do rules complicate matters for the business? *No!* A business system is no more complicated by having independent rules than are the games of chess, baseball, and football by having their own independent rulebooks.

Are rules all that matter? *Of course not!* Rather, rules simply need to be put on at least an equal footing with deliverables for addressing other needs, including process models, use cases, etc. These latter deliverables are needed to produce the raw power to do work — muscles for the business to flex. Rules represent a well-developed nervous system, a way to ensure your business works *smart*.

> Rules ensure your business works smart.

Summary

To conclude this discussion, let's revisit the question of how rules provide control and guidance in the business rule approach. In the human body, nerves connect to muscles, the source of power for behavior. The nerves control the muscles and, by that means, the resulting behavior. However, the nerves are not actually embedded within the muscles themselves.

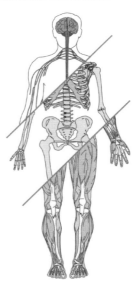

In a business rule system, rules are like the nerves. They connect to processes — the source of power for behavior. The rules control and guide the processes and, by that means, the resulting behavior. However, as we have discussed, the rules should not actually be embedded within the processes. This principle is called *Rule Independence.*

Processes connect to rules via events. Processes produce events, which can fire one or more rules. The rules may determine whether the event is undertaken correctly or will produce a desired outcome. The rules also may make some decision. The rules are externalized from the processes and established as a separate resource. This permits *direct* management of the rules, which in turn permits much closer tie-in to the business side.

This notion of *Rule Independence* is the centerpiece of the business rule approach. The various principles underlying this fundamental principle are enumerated in the *Business Rules Manifesto*[18], a copy of which can be found at the end of this book.

> Rule Independence is key.

Notes

¹ Since this discussion is informal, I will use the word *rule* instead of the more correct *rule statement* to refer to expressions of rules. The distinction is that the same rule can be given by statements in different forms and/or by statements in different languages (for example, French, Mandarin, and so on). In other words, there can be many different *rule statements* for exactly the same *rule*. I made the equivalent distinction in Chapter 1 between *expression of fact type and fact type*.

² As mentioned in Chapter 1, 'terms and facts' is a loose designation for a structured business vocabulary, often represented by a graphic fact model.

³ Refer to Chapters 8–12 in Ross [2003]. RuleSpeak® is a business rule notation developed by Business Rule Solutions, LLC (BRS) that has been used directly with hundreds of business people in numerous large-scale projects beginning in the mid-1990s. The sample rules above are expressed in RuleSpeak, as is the case for all other rules expressed in this book (unless noted otherwise).

⁴ More precisely, an *event* from this perspective can be defined as any change in state. However, this discussion is informal and such an exacting definition unnecessary here.

⁵ Except perhaps informally, based on interpersonal or intersystem messages.

⁶ I use the term *fire* in this discussion to mean loosely both *execute* (to evaluate the relevant condition[s]) and, if necessary, *invoke appropriate action*. In some rule technologies, *fire* is used to refer only to the latter.

⁷ The specific update event that poses a potential violation of the rule is actually the deletion of an instance for the 'is assigned to' fact type.

⁸ Rules do exist that are specific to individual update events, but these rules represent the exception, rather than the general case.

⁹ I mean *produces* in the sense of *can be analyzed to discover*.

¹⁰ An obvious exception is if the rule is qualified in such manner that it applies only when a given event occurs, for example: *A customer must be assigned to an agent who lives in the same city at the time of assignment.*

¹¹ That is, excluding rules that express logic for computations, inferences, and so on. Refer to Chapter 5 for additional discussion.

¹² Additional text can be provided, of course, to explain the relevance of the rule to the specific event, to suggest corrective measures, and so on.

¹³ In a truly *friendly* business rule system, when a rule is violated, a procedure or script can be made available to the user to assist in taking immediate corrective action. This opportunity is discussed in Chapter 6.

[14] In the categorization schemes presented in Chapter 5, these are called *operative rules* for the business perspective, and *rejectors* for the system perspective.

[15] For example, at each Business Rules Forum conference (http://www.BusinessRulesForum.com), successful real-world case studies are presented.

[16] Or use cases.

[17] This is also true for any prototype(s) in which users 'test-drive' new processes and procedures *before* implementation.

[18] Business Rules Group [2003].

Chapter 3

What the Business Manager Needs to Know

As a manager you want to know what the business rule approach means for your business. This chapter explains.

Lessons of a Legacy

As middle-level managers were eliminated in the downsizing and reengineerings of the 1980s and 1990s, they essentially took knowledge about many business rules with them. Indeed, we commonly now hear the complaint that the *systems* seem to be running the business.

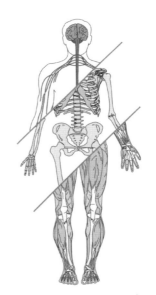

As a result, many companies today are facing tough choices in trying to regain that lost knowledge. One approach is to attempt to mine the business rules from the legacy code (not an easy prospect!). The alternative is either reengineering the business systems from scratch or replacing them with expensive (and often painful) deployments of packaged software. An important lesson can be learned from this: Never lose your business rules!

Never lose your business rules!

Any business initiative whose direct or indirect effect might be to eliminate human actors 'in the middle' should call on business rule techniques. Where else is this happening today? For one thing, we hear a lot about extended value chains crossing organizational boundaries between suppliers, producers, and customers. The real goal here is *compacting* the value chain, allowing direct, dynamic interaction between empowered actors anywhere along the way.

The implication is that certain types of organizational roles will be dramatically transformed or eliminated altogether. Can you see the parallel with reengineering? Before the target was middle-level managers. In the case of compacted value chains, the target is *middlemen*.[1]

Both of these roles (middle-level manager and middleman) served in times past not only to filter information — the responsibility commonly ascribed to them — but also to know and enforce business rules. Retaining their knowledge is crucial. The solution? Capturing and encoding their knowledge as business rules.

> **Business rules retain knowledge for the business.**

The Cost of Exceptions to Rules

When introduced to the business rule approach, the first reaction some people have is that their business has far more exceptions to rules than rules per se. They question how all these exceptions can be handled in any organized fashion. This is a valid concern.

The business rule approach treats exceptions to rules as merely more rules.[2] This treatment is crucial for a fundamental reason — one that touches on requirements development, on business process reengineering, and, indeed, on the business itself. Briefly, *rules cost something*.

> **All rules cost something.**

The most significant cost of rules is not the direct cost of their implementation and maintenance in business systems, especially using rule engines or decision management platforms. The real cost often lies hidden in the associated documentation, training, administration, and time — the time it takes to communicate the rules and the time it takes to change the rules. Time, of course, is among the most precious of all commodities. Your business does not need *more* rules — it probably needs fewer (*good*) rules!

> **Having fewer (good) rules is much better than having more rules.**

Chapter 3

Closing the Requirements Gap

As discussed in Chapter 2, the guidance messages that business workers see once an information/knowledge system is operational should be the very same business rules that knowledgeable workers on the business side gave *as requirements* during the earlier stages of the development project. Guidance messages, rule statements, rule-related requirements — these are all literally one and the same. Well-expressed rules during the requirements process mean well-expressed guidance messages; poorly-expressed rules during the requirements process mean poorly-expressed guidance messages.

Several observations about this principle are worth making. First, direct assistance in expressing the rules up front will prove extremely valuable to the managers and workers involved in rules capture. We see this as an important skill for business analysts. There is much more involved than simple wordsmithing.

Second is the potential for closing the requirements gap between the business side and the IT side that plagues many companies today. In traditional approaches, much is usually lost in the translation of up-front requirements to the actual running systems. In the business rule approach, the business side gets back whatever guidance it puts in — a truly *business*-oriented approach.

> The business rule approach helps to close the requirements gap.

Closing the Communications Gap

Ask managers and workers in the business what they mean by *requirements* for developing business systems, and typically you get answers centered on functions to be performed, or on the look and feel of how the system behaves through its interfaces (for example, graphical user interfaces). The answer "terms and facts" is almost never among the responses. Nonetheless, they are indeed a kind of requirement.

> Terms and facts are a type of requirement.

Terms and facts are by no means the *only* kind of requirement necessary for business system development, of course. Without them, however, you cannot provide real meaning or coherency (sense) to all the others, especially to the rules. For that reason, terms and facts probably represent the most *fundamental* kind of requirement.

Terms and facts literally do just that — they provide *meaning*. This meaning, of course, is abstract. It might not be as obvious as what a system does or how the system looks on the outside. Just because something is less obvious, however, does not mean it is any less important. Break a bone, and see what happens to the body's behavior!

> Terms and facts provide meaning and coherency
> to other kinds of requirements, especially rules.

The problem is by no means limited to communication of requirements between business workers and IT. Indeed, in many organizations today, business workers from different parts of the organization (e.g., different functional silos) often have trouble even talking to *each other*. Or to say this more accurately, they talk to each other, but they are not really *communicating*.

A well-managed, well-structured business vocabulary should be a central fixture of business operations. That means capturing business knowledge from the business-side workers and managers who possess it. The skills involved with distilling that business knowledge is essential for business analysts.[3] You will also need appropriate *business-level* platforms to support it.

> Your company needs business-level skills and resources
> for coordinating business vocabulary.

Chapter 3

Business-Level Platforms for Managing Business Rules

How many business rules does your company have? A hundred? A thousand? Ten thousand? More? How easy is it to change any one of those rules? How easy is it to determine where the rule is implemented? How easy is it to find out why it was implemented in the first place?

Many companies today are starting to realize they have significant problems with business rule management. Often, this perception did not start off that way. Initially, the perception might have fallen under some other label such as *change management, data quality, knowledge management,* or so on. Call it what you will, these companies are discovering that the business guidance at the core of their day-to-day operations is not being managed in any consistent or coherent manner.

Your company needs the right kind of business-level platform to manage its business rules.[4] What should such an automated work environment look like? What else should be recorded in it? What additional kinds of support are needed?

> Your company needs an automated business-level
> work environment for managing business rules.

Remember that business rules represent *business* guidance — not programming logic. The goal is to give *business* workers and/or *business* analysts the ability to manage and access the business guidance directly.[5] The focus should be on the kinds of challenges these business workers and analysts face on a day-in and day-out basis.

Fundamental in this regard is an *integrated* capability to manage business vocabulary and fact models. As discussed previously, when rules number in the thousands — or even 'just' in the hundreds — coordinating terminology is essential. Imagine trying to understand and apply that much business guidance without such coordination. It is hard to stress the need for business-level coordination of business vocabulary too much.

> Your automated business-level work environment
> for managing business rules must be
> integrated with business vocabulary and fact models.

Many questions about business rules that business workers and business analysts will have are quite predictable. Frequently asked questions include those below. Although the importance of these questions is self-evident, most companies have never managed this kind of core knowledge in any coordinated or comprehensive manner.

- To which areas of the business does a business rule apply?
- What work or decision-making task(s) does a business rule guide?
- Where is a business rule implemented?
- In what jurisdictions is a business rule enforced?
- What purpose does a business rule serve?
- When was a business rule created?
- When did a business rule become effective?
- Are there previous versions of a business rule?
- Is a business rule currently in effect?
- Has a business rule been retired or replaced, and if so, when and why?
- What influenced the creation or modification of a business rule?
- Who can answer particular kinds of questions about a business rule?
- Who has been involved with a business rule over time, and in what way?
- Where can more information about a business rule be found?
- Who is responsible for a business rule?

Another question crucial to managing business rules is being able to address relationships *between* business rules — that is, rule-to-rule connections. There are many ways in which business rules can be interconnected, the most important of which are those below. Being able to trace these relationships easily and reliably is also crucial to business rule management.

- A rule is an exception to another rule.
- A rule determines the applicable circumstances for another rule.
- A rule has been interpreted from or into another rule.

This last item is particularly important. Many business rules are interpretations of what we call *governing* rules — laws, acts, statutes, regulations, contracts, business policies, legal determinations, and so on. Knowing the *who, when* and *why* of such interpretations is crucial in supporting impact assessment when the rules change — which nearly all rules do, sooner or later!

In today's world, this 'history' (let's call it *corporate memory*) is unfortunately very costly or even impossible to discover or reproduce. Even worse, once discovered or reproduced for a particular need at a point in time, it is often not retained in any organized fashion for future use. That means the whole process must be repeated the next time it is needed, *ad nauseum*.

Clearly, this is a very expensive way to do business, not to mention the risks of getting it wrong each time. The valuable resources this rework consumes could certainly be put to better use in other areas. Think of business rule management as a practical means to retain *corporate memory*.[6]

> Business rule management is about retaining corporate memory.

All the listed items illustrate various forms of *traceability*. Predefined reports and queries provide many kinds of basic support for this crucial area. Beyond that, visualization techniques are quite useful for presenting more complex or highly-interrelated information. Comprehensive support for rule traceability is a key ingredient in successful business rule management.

> Your automated business-level work environment
> for managing business rules
> must provide comprehensive traceability.

Another important aspect of business rule management is the difficulty of validating large sets of rules, and ensuring that the business guidance is complete, internally consistent, and non-redundant. Automated support in this area is a *must have*. Examples of *rule quality* items:[7]

- A rule is similar to another rule.

- A rule subsumes another rule.

- A rule is semantically equivalent to another rule.

- A rule is in conflict with another rule.

Rather than a new chore for the company's thinly stretched resources, such support should be viewed as an important new area of opportunity. Never before has the company's business guidance been in a form that could be checked *before deployment* for true quality by business workers and business analysts from the business point of view.

> Your automated business-level work environment
> for managing business rules
> must provide automated quality assessment
> for use by business workers and business analysts.

One way or another, every company will eventually discover the need for business rule management. To support it, new skills must be acquired and new work environments implemented. Fortunately, pioneering companies have already discovered what these techniques are, and good commercial tools have emerged to support them.[8] These tools and techniques are *already* paying off handsomely.

Other Kinds of Business Requirements

As discussed earlier, terms, facts and rules *do not* cover all kinds of business requirements, nor do they eliminate the need to model certain other fundamental aspects of the business. They do, however, complement and sharpen the other needed models, including:

Business Strategy: Before undertaking a project to (re-)engineer some business capability, even one that will not involve automation, the prudent course is to create a battle plan identifying the key elements of the business solution (including core business rules). Such a battle plan is *not* the same as developing the business case or the project plan. For excellent insight about business strategy in the context of business/IT requirements, refer to Lam [1998], and the Business Rules Group [2005].

Business Process: A business process model is an end-to-end, result-oriented view of the business tasks appropriate for a planned, optimal response to a significant business event. Performing these tasks produces and 'consumes' information and knowledge. Business rules externalize the guidance for such activity, but in most cases, do *not* substitute for the business processes themselves. Refer to Chapter 6 for discussion.[9]

Real-Time Knowledge Delivery

Point-of-Sale (POS) is a familiar notion in the world of commerce. A well-engineered experience at the point-of-sale has obvious benefits both for the customer — a positive buying experience — and for the business of the supplier — real-time intelligence about sales volume, cash flow, buying trends, inventory depletion, customer profiles, etc. Is there a similar customer/supplier event for knowledge workers? If so, how are business rules involved?

An equivalent customer-supplier event exists within a business concerning knowledge — particularly guidance and know-how (business rules). I call this critical event *point-of-knowledge* (POK).

In the world of commerce, we often say that customer and supplier are *parties* to POS events. Each of us is a customer in some POS events, and many of us act as suppliers in others. The same is true about POK events. Each of us is a 'customer' of knowledge in some POK events, and many of us act as 'suppliers' in others. Sometimes we switch roles within  minutes or even seconds. For POK events, at least one of the parties is always a *knowledge worker*; often both of the parties are.

Much has been written about the emergence of the role of *knowledge worker*. Far less, however, is understood about the engineering of effective POKs. This is where the business rule approach comes to bear.

I should clarify that POK events are *not* the kind that occur in rapid, collaborative development — for example, in the cultivation of customer prospects, or in the engineering of complex product/services. You would not use Lotus Notes or other such knowledge messaging/retention tools to support POKs. Instead, POKs represent the events where corporate guidance (a.k.a., business rules) are developed, applied, assessed, and ultimately retired. In other words, POKs are really about corporate governance and the application of the company's specialized know-how.

The customer/supplier 'experience' at POK events is crucial to worker productivity and job satisfaction. In no small measure, this is the real challenge of POK support. After all, the product/service for POKs is *knowledge* — something you cannot carry in your hands. Some of the most important critical success criteria in engineering POKs are the following.

- All communication in a POK must be in the language of the business, not IT.

- Interactions in each POK must be gauged to the knowledge level (and authorization) of the individual parties.

- Less-experienced workers fulfilling the supplier role in a POK must be enabled to perform at the level of the company's most experienced workers. (Remember that in a world of constant change, even the organization's best workers are frequently thrown into time-sensitive roles for which they are not fully prepared. Chapter 6 calls this *time shock.*)

- The guidance and know-how (business rules) relevant to any given POK must be presented and/or applied in a succinct, highly-selective fashion.

- The guidance and know-how (business rules) must also be presented and/or applied in a *timely* fashion (i.e., 'just-in-time') to accommodate fast-paced refinement and change in business policies and practices.

- POK-support platforms must be in the form of *knowledge companions*, enabling never-ending, on-the-job training of the knowledge workers.[10]

> **Your company needs run-time platforms to support POKs.**

Chapter 3

Well-engineered POK support platforms[11] also have obvious benefits for the business of the supplier — for example, real-time intelligence about the 'hit' rate of rules, patterns of evolving customer (and supplier) behavior, emergence of compliance risks, and so on. [12] The business rule approach is clearly how to get your company to the real point of knowledge!

Your run-time POK platform should support
knowledge activity monitoring.

Summary

This discussion has reviewed some of the business problems that the business rule approach addresses. Other crucial problems for organizations today include business and software adaptability, compliance, mass customization, and more, all of which have been addressed successfully using the business rule approach.[13] Given the challenges in businesses today, business rules are simply inevitable.

Business rules are inevitable.

Notes

[1]   Sometimes called *disintermediation.*

[2]   Refer to Chapter 5 for discussion.

[3]   For excellent insight into the role of business analyst, see Seer [2002].

[4]   At the risk of oversimplifying, the literal specification of rules is just data, so in essence *automated* simply means *databasing* the rules. In other words, business rules should be stored in an automated facility or repository (we prefer the term 'central guidance store') where they can be managed and readily accessed.

[5]   You should consider very carefully whether current commercial rule engine or repository offerings measure up in this regard. Unfortunately, most were engineered for primary use by IT staff. The difference is not a trivial one.

[6]   And with the proper coordination, establishing a measure of *accountability.*

[7]   Refer to Chapter 5 for a more complete discussion.

[8]   RuleXpress, offered by RuleArts, LLC, is a best-of-breed example. Refer to http://www.RuleArts.com for current information.

[9]   For excellent insight into modeling and managing business processes, refer to Burlton [2001].

[10]   Refer to Chapter 6 for additional discussion.

[11]   Rule engines and decision management platforms can support this need.

[12]   KAM, the counterpart of BAM (*business activity monitoring*). Again, rule engines and decision management platforms can support this need.

[13]   Refer to Chapters 1–4 of Ross [2003] for a more comprehensive discussion.

Part 2

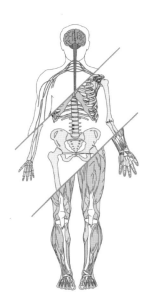

Concepts of the Business Rule Approach for the Practitioner

Chapter 4

A Closer Look at Fact Models

Chapter 1 discussed how structure — that is, terms and facts — is treated in the business rule approach. The objective is an agreed business vocabulary, including its representation as a fact model. Just in case I need to say this: There should be only a single fact model[1] for the entire scope of the business capacity.[2]

A structured business vocabulary captures what people mean when they talk about basic operational knowledge and business know-how. What does *basic* mean? *Basic* means that the knowledge cannot be derived or computed from any other knowledge. A fact model is therefore the crucial starting point for developing more advanced forms of business knowledge, including measures and rules.

This chapter expands on the discussion of fact modeling in Chapter 1. It is intended for business people and business analysts wanting a more complete understanding.[3] In fact modeling, everything eventually comes around to developing good definitions, so let's start with that.

Forming Definitions

A central idea of the business rule approach is that any aspect of business guidance or know-how that might change should be treated as rules. In forming definitions, therefore, the practitioner should always focus on what is unlikely to ever change — that is, on the fundamental *essence* of business concepts.

> In defining business concepts, focus on essence.

For example, consider the following definition of *customer* proposed by a practitioner in a real-life project.

Customer: *an organization or individual person that has placed at least one paid order during the previous two years*[4]

Areas of business practice that could change over time are:

- That a customer may be *either* an organization or an individual person.
- That *placing orders* is the core criteria for being a customer.
- That a minimum of exactly *one* order is a criterion for being a customer.
- That an order having been *paid* is a criterion for being a customer.
- That the timeframe of exactly *two* years is a criterion for being a customer.

Now consider the Webster's definition of 'customer'.[5]

Customer: *one that purchases some commodity or service; especially one that purchases systematically or frequently*

In contrast to the practitioner's definition, the Webster's version is clearly an *essence definition* and is therefore much better. The embedded business practices of the practitioner's definition should be treated as forms of guidance, as follows.

Rule: *A customer always places at least one paid order during the previous two years.*[6]

Clarification: *A customer may be an organization or individual person.*

> Business guidance subject to change should be treated as business rules.

Forming Fact Types

At its core, a fact model is about fundamental relations between business concepts, stripped of quantification and qualification. Consider the rule from above: *A customer always places at least one paid order during the previous two years.* The fundamental relation between the two central concepts, customer and order, is *places*. The appropriate fact type for the fact model then is *customer places order*.[7] That really gets down to *barebones* knowledge! In arriving at the fact type, we stripped away the following:

Chapter 4

Quantification: *at least one* [paid] order

Qualifications: *paid* order; places … *during the previous two years*

> Fact types represent barebones knowledge.

Graphically, the fact type would be represented as in Figure 4–1.[8]

Figure 4–1. Graphic representation of a fact type.

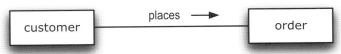

A key question in fact modeling is whether two candidate fact types mean the same thing or something different.   Usually, but not always, the answer is obvious.   For example, *order is placed by customer* is obviously just a different wording for the fact type meant by *customer places order.*[9]

Should the second wording be included in the fact model? In practice, the answer has to do with scaling up. In the early stages of fact model development, additional wordings are not really necessary. Later on, as the number of business rules grows, additional wordings become increasingly important. The reason is simply that some (probably many) business rules are likely to require the additional wordings.

For example, consider the business rule: *A rush order that is placed by a high-risk customer must be paid in advance.* Since the two wordings in question are for the same fact type, a new connection (line) in the fact model should *not* be included. Figure 4–2 illustrates how the additional wording would be indicated.

Figure 4–2. A fact type with two wordings.

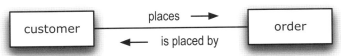

Sometimes, it is not as obvious as in the example that two wordings share the same meaning. Consider *household includes person* and *person belongs to household.* Same meaning? Probably,[10] although unlike *places* and *is placed [by]* in the previous example, *includes* and *belongs [to]* are not merely different forms of the same verb. Assuming that only a single fact type is represented, the wordings should be indicated as in Figure 4–3.

Figure 4–3. A fact type with two wordings that use different verbs.

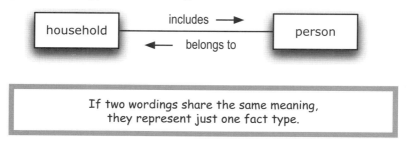

If two wordings share the same meaning,
they represent just one fact type.

Roles

Business people often have special
terms for a concept that they use only
in the context of some particular fact
type. For example, in the fact type just
discussed, business people are likely
to say *household includes <u>household
member</u>* and *<u>household member</u> belongs
to household*. We know, however, that

household member is simply a special name given to a *person* in the context
of a household. A term such as *household member* is called a *role*[11] and is
graphically indicated as in Figure 4–4.

Figure 4–4. A role in the context of a fact type.

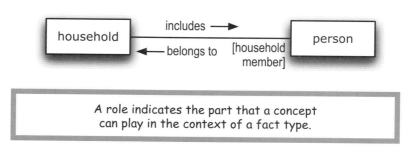

A role indicates the part that a concept
can play in the context of a fact type.

Roles are an important means of capturing additional business vocabulary
in an integrated, non-disruptive manner.[12] That's important, because
scaling up to large numbers of rules depends on the precision and
completeness of the underlying vocabulary.

Chapter 4

Creating the Fact Model: Case Study

A simple case study illustrates how development of fact models typically proceeds. Consider a university that provides adult education, offering a variety of courses organized into workshop sessions. A first fact type for the university fact model might be *workshop session [meeting] is held for course offering*, as illustrated in Figure 4–5.

Figure 4–5. A first fact type for the university fact model.

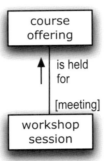

A second fact type might be *student enrolls in course offering*, as indicated in Figure 4–6.

Figure 4–6. Adding a second fact type to the university fact model.

Note that no dependencies are assumed to exist between the two fact

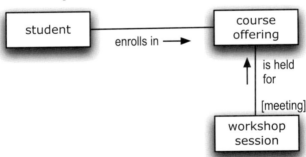

types; in other words, an instance of each can stand on its own. By *stand on its own* I mean:

- An instance of *student enrolls in course offering* can exist:
  - independently of whether any meeting is held for that course offering.
  - *before* a meeting is held for that course offering.

- An instance of *workshop session [meeting] is held for course offering* can exist:
  - independently of whether any student enrolls in that course offering.
  - *before* any student enrolls in that course offering.

To continue, suppose the university has a business practice not to hold (or even schedule) a meeting for a course offering unless a certain number of students actually enroll for it. (Sounds reasonable!) Such a business practice should be expressed as a *rule* — for example: *A meeting may be held for a course offering only if at least 5 students are enrolled for the course offering.*[13] Fact types simply provide a blueprint for the basic knowledge needed to capture and support such business practices.

> **Fact types provide a knowledge blueprint for business practices expressed as rules.**

Students enrolled in a course offering that has sufficient enrollment might attend some, but not all, of the workshop sessions for that course offering. Assuming the university deems knowing about actual attendance important, we need a third fact type *student attends workshop session* as indicated in Figure 4–7.

Figure 4–7. Adding a third fact type to the university fact model.

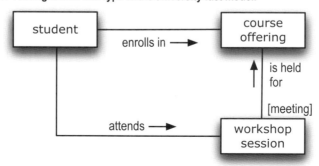

Does the university permit a student to attend a workshop session for a course offering in which the student is *not* enrolled? *Probably not.* (As always, the answer depends on its specific business practices.) Assuming the answer is *no*, the following additional rule should be specified: *A student may attend a workshop session only if the student enrolls in the course offering for which the workshop session is a meeting.* Note how (as always) the rule builds on the fact types in the fact model. Two fact types are referenced directly: *student attends workshop session* and *student enrolls in course offering.* The third fact type — *workshop session is held for course offering* — is referenced indirectly, via the role *meeting.* A workshop session can be a meeting only if the workshop session is actually held for a course offering.

Grades are another obvious concern for the university (and students!). How are *grades* handled in the fact model?

A *grade* (for clarity, let's call it *grade earned*) is specific to a *given* student in a *given* course offering for which he/she is enrolled. It is important to notice that a *grade earned* is not about either the student on his/her own or the course offering on its own. In other words, *grade earned* is about the relation between *student* and *course offering* — that is, *grade earned* pertains to (is a *property* of) the fact type *student enrolls in course offering.* (More about properties later.)

In fact modeling, only 'things' can have properties, not the relations between them (i.e., not fact types). The solution is to convert the fact type into a 'thing'; in other words, to *objectify* (or *reify*) it. In English we do this all the time simply by giving names to relations (fact types). For example, the fact type *student enrolls in course offering* might be called *enrollment.* Because enrollment is a thing, it *can* have a property.

To diagram what I just described requires visualizing the transformation of the fact type into a thing. In Figure 4–8 this transformation[14] is illustrated using a dashed line.[15] Now *grade earned* can be indicated for *enrollment.*

Figure 4–8. Objectifying a fact type.

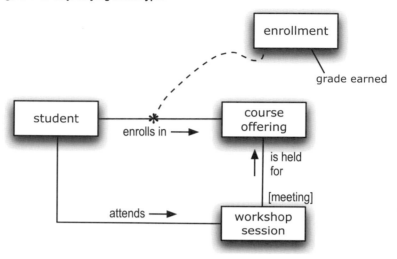

> Noun-type concepts can have properties;
> verb-type concepts cannot
> because they are merely verbal connectors.

Here's a quick summary of the results from our analysis of the university knowledge structure. The fact model currently includes:

- Concepts about four kinds of 'thing' — represented by the terms *student, course offering, workshop session,* and *enrollment.* Each of these things can have properties and participate in other fact types.

- Two additional concepts — represented by the terms *meeting* (a role) and *grade earned* (a property). These things cannot have properties or participate in other fact types.

- Four fact types —
    o   *workshop session [meeting] is held for course offering*
    o   *student enrolls in course offering*
    o   *student attends workshop session*
    o   *enrollment has grade earned*

- One objectification — the fact type *student enrolls in course offering* has been objectified as *enrollment.*

Something this case study does not illustrate very well is the *size* of a typical structured business vocabulary. Fact models can easily grow into the hundreds of terms. For fact models to *scale up,* you need an automated workstation, which must provide techniques for managing meaningful vocabulary subsets.[16]

> ## You need an automated business-level
> ## work environment that can support large fact models.

Unary and N-ary Fact Types

Since each of the four fact types in the case study involves exactly two terms, each is a *binary* fact type. The central fact types of a fact model are always *binary*. Other fact types, however, can be *unary* (that is, involve only one term) or *n-ary* (that is, involve more than two terms).

To illustrate, suppose a company builds and markets complex products. Owing to the products' costs and complexity, the company focuses its resources carefully on products being actively marketed. Also, the company's sales representatives often receive special briefings about some specific product by some knowledgeable engineer. At least the following two kinds of knowledge are therefore required:

- To know whether a product is being actively marketed.
- To know which engineer briefs which sales representative about which product.

Note that the former item mentions only a single term, *product*. The fact type *product is being actively marketed* is therefore *unary*. The second item mentions three: *product, engineer,* and *sales representative*. The fact type *engineer briefs sales representative about product* is therefore *n-ary*. Figure 4–9 illustrates how these two fact types can be represented in a fact model.

Figure 4–9. Representing unary and n-ary fact types.

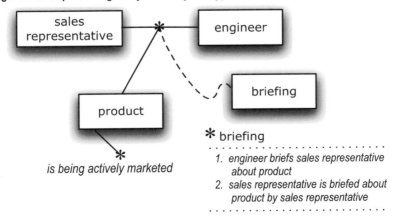

* briefing
. . . .
1. *engineer briefs sales representative about product*
2. *sales representative is briefed about product by sales representative*
. . . .

The asterisk symbol appearing for both fact types in figure 4–9 is always used for unary and n-ary fact types.[17] The asterisk indicates that some special wording for the fact type is required.

- As illustrated by figure 4–9, the wording for a unary fact type appears close to a thin connection line. A unary fact type always provides a simple *yes-or-no* answer.[18] The unary fact type *product is being actively marketed* indicates that a given product either *is or is not* being actively marketed.[19] Such knowledge is often relevant to rules — for example: *A briefing may be only for a product that is actively marketed.*[20]

- The n-ary fact type *engineer briefs sales representative about product* cannot be worded in a practical, unambiguous manner using the three connection lines intersecting at the asterisk. (Try it. Note that a second wording is *sales representative is briefed about product by engineer.* That one — and any others — must be worked in too.) So the wordings are annotated separately, as is convenient in the layout of the diagram.[21] Sometimes, that might be at some distance away.[22]

Elementary Fact Types

Every *associative* fact type in a fact model (i.e., each fact type that includes two or more terms) should be *elementary*. *Elementary* means it should not be possible to break the fact type down into two or more other fact types, each with fewer terms, without losing knowledge.

> A fact model should include only elementary fact types.

For example, suppose a briefing were set up about multiple products, and/or to brief multiple sales representatives, and/or to be given by multiple engineers. In that case, a briefing is not always selective to a particular *combination* of engineer, sales representative, and product. Replacing the n-ary fact type by two or three individual fact types (as appropriate), each with only two terms, would not risk losing anything (i.e., any selective knowledge). By the way, elementary fact types having three terms, and especially ones with four or more terms, are *rare* for basic business operations and know-how.

Moreover, a business should be concerned with establishing a *stable* knowledge blueprint, taking a long-term view of potential changes in business practice. Consider the three-termed fact type *engineer briefs sales representative about product*. It certainly seems plausible that at some point in the future (even if not currently) the business will want to set up a briefing about multiple products, and/or to brief multiple sales representatives, and/or to be given by multiple engineers.

The safest approach (i.e., the approach most accommodating of future changes) is therefore the following:

- Make *briefing* a term in its own right, not simply an objectification.
- Include three binary fact types in the fact model: *briefing is given to sales representative*; *briefing is given by engineer*; and *briefing covers product*.
- Specify one or more rules if current business practice limits briefings to at most one sales representative, and/or one engineer, and/or one product.

In other words, the best approach is to *generalize* the fact model as much as is reasonable,[23] letting rules handle current and/or future business practices.

> Generalize the fact model as much as is reasonable;
> handle more restrictive business practices
> — current or future — using rules.

Factual Connection Templates

The focus of this chapter so far has been primarily on fact types whose shape (business meaning) lies completely with the factual sentence forms (wordings) supplied for them by business workers and/or business analysts. The fact types have no implicit or prefabricated meaning of any kind.

Other important kinds of fact types come in *pre-defined* shapes that reflect specific kinds of logical connections that people make in operating the business or applying its know-how. As introduced in Chapter 1, each of these shapes — called a *factual connection template* — takes a form  that can be worded using pre-defined factual sentence forms. The kinds of statements that can be made with these templates and forms are powerful. The remainder of this chapter illustrates the use of four of these forms, as presented in Table 4–1.

Table 4–1. Examples of Factual Connection Templates.

Kind of Factual Connection Template [24]	Pre-defined Factual Sentence Form	Example	Sample Statement
property	(thing) *has* (thing)	order *has* date taken order *has* date promised	An order's date promised must be at least 24 hours after the order's date taken.
categorization	(class of thing) *is a category of* (class of thing)	'corporate customer' *is a category of* 'customer' 'rush shipment' *is a category of* 'shipment'	A rush shipment may include only orders placed by a corporate customer.
composition (whole–part or partitive)	(whole) *consists of* (parts)	chair *consists of*: • legs • seat • back • armrests	A chair may be ordered without armrests.
assortment	(thing) *is an instance of* (class of thing)	Canada *is an instance of* country Canadian dollar *is an instance of* currency	An order may be priced using the currency Canadian dollar only if the customer placing the order is located in Canada.

Categories and Categorizations

A category is a class of things whose meaning is more restrictive than, but otherwise compliant with, some other class of things. For example, *male* is a category of *person*. Each male is always a person, but has additional properties that other males have, but not all people have. In general, a category represents a kind or variation within a more general concept. Creating one or more categories is called *categorization*. The terms used for categorizations expand the business vocabulary in important ways, especially (but not exclusively) for expressing rules precisely.

> Categories are kinds or variations of a more general concept
> that are significant to the business.

Categories are abundant in business operations and/or know-how. Figure 4–10 illustrates several categories (using heavy lines) that are relevant to the *briefing* example.

The following *categorizations* are illustrated by Figure 4–10.

- Both *sales representative* and *engineer* are recognized as categories of a new, more general concept *employee*. Note the property *employee name* indicated for *employee*. Since all sales representatives and engineers can have names — indeed, *any* employee can — the *name* property is indicated only for *employee*. Remember that all sales representatives and engineers *are* employees (in this business), so the *name* property pertains as a matter of course to both *representative* and *engineer*. It does not need to be re-specified for them.[25] On the other hand, commission rates apparently pertain only to sales representatives — not to all employees (e.g., not to engineers) — since *commission rate* is indicated only for *sale representative*.

- *Product* now has three categories — *military*, *corporate*, and *consumer* — forming a group. (This group of categories is named *orientation* — more about that later.[26]) Note that (as always for categories) *military*, *corporate* and *consumer* must be products. Indeed, unless everyone reading the diagram is thoroughly familiar with categorization, better labels would probably be *military product*, *corporate product,* and *consumer product.*[27]

> Be mindful of the more general concept
> in naming or interpreting a category.

Figure 4–10. Illustration of categories.

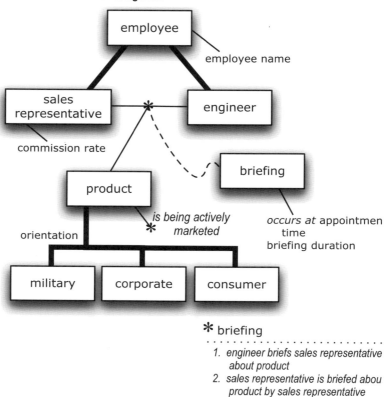

$*$ briefing
. . . .
1. *engineer briefs sales representative about product*
2. *sales representative is briefed abou product by sales representative*
. . . .

Properties

Figure 4–10 also provides an opportunity to examine properties more closely. According to Webster's,[28] a property (in the sense appropriate for fact modeling) is a quality or trait belonging to a person or thing; an attribute, characteristic, or distinguishing mark common to all members of a class or species.[29] As previously mentioned, *employee name* is a property of *employee*, and *commission rate* is a property of *sales representative*. In Figure 4–10, a thin line is used to attach each of these properties to the appropriate box (term).

Exactly what does this thin line represent? The thin line actually represents a binary fact type based on the factual connection template for properties. The predefined factual sentence form for this template defaults to *(thing) has (thing)*. The important word in this form is *has*. The verb *to have* is very general — not specific or descriptive at all. *Has* makes for very poor wording of associative fact types that are not specified as properties. For properties, on the other hand, a *has* default is quite convenient. In such cases, the real meaning of the fact type is bound up with, and conveyed sufficiently by, its being a property, so *has* is generally adequate.

> A property implies a binary fact type
> in which one thing is closely tied
> to the meaning or understanding of another.

Can properties be worded using verbs other than *has*? *Yes.* For example, the *commission rate* property of *sales representative* might be worded *sales representative is compensated at commission rate.*[30]

The term listed at the end of the line (i.e., the property) is often actually a role. For example:

- Suppose commission rates are always percentages (in this business). Then the *commission rate* property of *sales representative* actually represents the fact type *sales representative is compensated at [commission rate] percentage.*

- Similarly, the *employee name* property of employee might actually represent the fact type *employee has [employee name] name.*

Why bother with a graphic shorthand for properties? The answer again has to do with scaling up. If you were to treat all properties as 'regular' associative fact types, the fact model would become hopelessly cluttered with connections having to do with such things as percentages and other kinds of numbers, names, dates, units of measure, and much more. These connections are of secondary importance to the business. Avoid that![31]

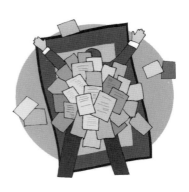

> Reduce clutter in the fact model to focus attention
> on the fact types of primary concern to the business.

Figure 4–10 actually includes several other properties, as follows.

- The n-ary fact type *engineer briefs sales representative about product* is objectified (or reified) as *briefing* (as earlier). Two properties for *briefing* have been indicated using a *single* thin line (another shorthand to reduce clutter).[32] The first, which assumes the default verb *has*, would be fully expressed as *briefing has [briefing duration] elapsed time*. The second, which includes the explicit wording *occurs at*, would be fully expressed as *briefing occurs at [appointment time] date-time*.

- Note *orientation* just above the crossbar for the categorization of *product*. *Orientation* is an example of special kind of property that names a group of two or more categories for a class of things organized using a common categorization scheme.[33] An example of an organized group of categories familiar to us all is *male* and *female*, which we call *gender* (not shown in the diagram). *Gender* is a property of *person*; therefore we can say *person has gender*. Similarly, *orientation* is a property of *product*; therefore we say *product has orientation*. Is it required that every product fall into at least one of the three categories, *military*, *government*, and *consumer*? (Or perhaps into *exactly* one?) Don't assume so — that would require some explicit rule(s). As always, fact models presume the general case — current or future business practices should be represented as rules.

Compositions — Whole–Part (Partitive) Connections

Many things in the real world are composites, made up of several other kinds of thing. For example, an automobile (simplistically) is composed of an engine, a body, and wheels. A mechanical pencil is made up of a

barrel, a lead-advance mechanism, lead (refill), and eraser (refill).[34] An address is made up of a street number, a street, an apartment number, a city, a state/province, a country, and a zip code / postal code.

Sorting out the terminology and composition of such *whole–part* connections is often quite useful. Before looking at a graphic example, here are several relevant questions and answers:

- Is every instance of the whole in a whole–part connection required to have at least one instance of each part? *No.* For example, not every address has an apartment number. A rule must be given to indicate which part(s) every instance of the whole is required to have.
- Can an instance of a whole have more than one instance of a kind of part? *Yes.* An automobile must have at least three wheels (a rule).
- Can the specification of a whole–part connection indicate only one kind of part? *Yes.* However, exercise common sense![35]
- Can a part itself be a whole composed of other parts? *Yes.* Multiple levels of composition are possible.
- Can both the whole and the parts be selectively involved in fact types on their own? *Yes.*

- Can an instance of a part exist independently from an instance of the whole? *Yes* (unless rules disallow it). A wheel, for example, can be removed from an automobile.
- Can an instance of a part be in more than one instance of a whole at the same time? *Yes* (again, unless rules disallow it). A power source, for example, can be part of more than one circuit.

> Whole–part connections permit capture of
> terms involved in composition.

Figure 4–11 provides a diagrammatic example. Thin lines portray the composition of *briefing* which, using the appropriate predefined factual sentence form, is expressed as *briefing is composed of: introduction, main body, conclusion.* By the way, this structure applies whether or not *briefing* results from objectification.

Figure 4–11. Example of a composition.

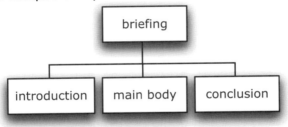

Assortments

A central focus in fact modeling is on identifying (and naming) the classes of things important to basic operations and/or know-how of the business. Most often the business cannot possibly know in advance what all the instances of a class of things will be. For example, most businesses cannot predict all their future customers.

For certain classes of things, however, the business can identify and/or prescribe in advance some or all of the instances of a class of things. For example, we know all the European countries at the present time. Moreover, the business may have many rules that pertain selectively to one or more of these instance-level things. For example, a business might have the rule: *A shipment may be made only to the European countries United Kingdom and Netherlands.*

Connecting an instance to its particular class of things is called *assortment.* This is an important additional area that business vocabularies often must cover. Figure 4–12 illustrates diagrammatic representation of an assortment. The double wavy line[36] indicates an assortment connection from the class of things *European Country* to some of its instances (not all).[37]

Figure 4–12. Example of assortment.

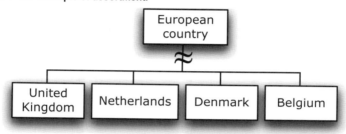

Here are additional examples of assortments:

- *Health care:* All recognized health services — for example, *consultation, office visit, hospital admission, surgery,* and so on.

- *Ship inspection:* All recognized parts of a ship — for example, *bulkhead, hatch cover, railing, deck,* and so on.

These examples were chosen deliberately to illustrate an important point about assortments, especially as they relate to business rules — assortments can be multi-level. For example, the instances *bulkhead, hatch cover,* etc. of the class of things *ship part type* (very numerous!) might themselves be viewed as classes of things with respect to the *specific* bulkheads, hatch covers, etc. (probably with serial numbers[38]) actually found on a given ship or in a given shipyard. The rules of interest to the business might be targeted toward any of the levels.

> Assortments permit capture of instance-level terms
> that can be known or prescribed in advance
> of actual business activity.

Chapter 4

Summary

A fact model represents a structured business vocabulary, a blueprint of the basic knowledge pertaining to operational business processes and know-how. A fact model is essential for scaling up to large numbers of rules, as well as for more effective specification of other kinds of requirements.

Developing a fact model has an important additional benefit. Inevitably, it helps bring into clear relief alternative ideas about how the business capacity itself can be best structured to satisfy business goals. When and by whom should such issues be resolved? These are clearly issues that should be resolved by business-side workers and managers *before* the project moves into system design or coding.

Unfortunately, many business-side workers and managers have been intimidated in the past by data models, class diagrams, and similar artifacts. I want to emphasize that there is no need whatsoever to view a fact model as representing anything technical.[39] If you have the relevant business knowledge, a fact model should never be hard to understand. If it is, somebody is simply doing something wrong! Remember, it's simply terms and facts — what the people mean when they *communicate* about basic things of the business.

> A fact model is ultimately about
> improving basic business communication.

Notes

1   A fact model can be rendered into selective *views*, of course, for different audiences. Also, I will comment in these notes on the notion of *neighborhoods*, a technique BRS has used successfully for partitioning the visualization of large business vocabularies.

2   Again, *business capacity* usually refers to some meaningful subset of the business.

3   Fact modeling has a long pedigree. A pioneer in this area is Terry Halpin and his Object Role Modeling (ORM) approach. Refer to Halpin [2001]. ORM in turn had its roots in Shir Nijssen's NIAM (Natural Language Information Analysis Model) developed in the mid 1970s.

4   Notice there is no period at the end of the definition. This omission is intentional, reflecting standard dictionary practice. (Check Webster's to confirm that for yourself!) Briefly, the reason is that a definition should be viewed as a phrase or expression that can be substituted for the corresponding term in any sentence (e.g., any rule) where the term appears, without any change in the meaning of the sentence. Of course, such substitution would produce rather long sentences, but the notion does serve to ensure the fitness (or literally the 'fit') of each definition.

5   *Merriam-Webster's Unabridged Dictionary*, 2000, definition 2a.

6   A good business rule analyst would then ask about the specific criteria (dates) for how to determine *previous two years*.

7   *Customer places order* is actually a factual sentence form, rather than fact type *per se*. Strictly speaking, a fact type is purely conceptual. As mentioned in Chapter 1, a factual sentence form represents (i.e., provides the a wording for) a fact type, just as a term is a word or word phrase that represents (stands for) a concept. However, the discussion that follows is not meant to be formal, so this distinction will be ignored except where doing so might cause confusion.

8   The graphic notation presented in this chapter is called FACT™ (*Factual Connections & Templates*). FACT notation was developed in large-scale client projects by BRS starting in the mid-1990s. FACT notation is consistent with, and provides a business-friendly face to, *SBVR* [2005].

9   The two wordings express only one underlying meaning. Literally, these are two ways to express (call out) the same 'semantic'.

10 A relevant test would be the following. Does *person is included in household* always involve exactly the same individual real-world connections (instances) as *person belongs to household?* Probably so. The same is also probably true for *household includes person*. So probably these are three wordings for a single fact type.

11 The sense of *role* as used here carries the usual meaning: *a part being played* by something, *a function assumed* by something, or *a selective*

usage of something *in a particular situation.* In the context of fact types, however, the intended sense for *role* is more accurately stated: *it can be known that* something *can* play a part, assume a function, or be used in a selective way in a particular situation. Remember that fact models are always about knowledge, not actions.

¹² Roles are a particularly good way to handle terms that simply reflect the wording of a fact type. For example, consider the fact type *party [insured] is insured by policy. Insured* simply reflects the wording *is insured by.* Or *person [owner] owns vehicle. Owner* simply reflects the wording *owns.* Note that 'insured' and 'owner' are *not* merely synonyms of 'party' and 'person', respectively. To be a synonym, a term must mean *exactly* the same thing as another term. The practical test for *exactly the same thing* is whether each term could be substituted for the other term in any statement (e.g., rules) that references the underlying concept. That is certainly not the case for *insured* and *party*, and *owner* and *person,* respectively.

One caveat: if a term seems to represent a concept that has its *own* properties — properties that can be talked about *independently* of the context of a given fact type — then the term should not be treated as a role. Instead, the term should be treated as a *category*. More about that later.

¹³ The rule might instead be: *A course offering must be cancelled if fewer than 5 students enroll in it. Cancelled* would represent a state of *course offering.* States are handled in fact models by specifying either categories or unary fact types. See later discussion of these fact-modeling notions. By the way, a good rule analyst always questions *time* — in this case, *when* should the course offering be cancelled?

¹⁴ i.e., *objectification* or *reification*

¹⁵ Since the fact model represents knowledge, not actions, it is more accurate to say that the dotted line represents the knowledge that *results* from the objectification (transformation).

¹⁶ In FACT notation, subsets of a fact model are called *neighborhoods.*

¹⁷ The asterisk is standard FACT notation. An asterisk may also be used for binary fact types, but can be omitted (as in the earlier diagrams) unless specifically needed for objectifying (reifying) the fact type, possibly to show some property(ies).

¹⁸ That is, a unary fact type is always Boolean-valued.

¹⁹ In other words, the unary fact type indicates whether a given product either is or is not in the *state* of being actively marketed. As mentioned earlier, unary fact types are often used to define states.

²⁰ A good rule analyst would immediately follow-up on any criteria (rules) concerning *actively marketed.*

[21] Objectification is not mandatory in FACT notation.

[22] Ambiguity rarely arises even if multiple fact types appear on the diagram with asterisks. The associated wordings must match the terms connected into the asterisk *exactly* in name and number. In the rare case that ambiguity does arise, subscripts for the asterisks can be included.

[23] *Reasonable* here means that chance of a business practice changing is not negligible.

[24] Following *SBVR* [2005].

[25] *Inheritance* of the property is assumed.

[26] The three boxes 'coming together' under *product* merely indicates there is some meaning in the grouping with respect to *orientation*. The notation does *not* imply any embedded rule (e.g., mutual exclusivity). More later.

[27] The boxes represent that *anyway* — these labels simply emphasize the point.

[28] *Merriam-Webster's Unabridged Dictionary*, 2000, definitions 1a and 1d(1).

[29] The appropriate sense for business rules is that any member of the class of things *can* have an instance of the property. A rule is required if each member *must* have one.

[30] FACT notation for a property with an explicit wording is exactly the same as for any other associative fact type. For example, the wording *is compensated at* would be shown with a directional arrow close to the thin line to the property *commission rate*.

[31] Separate neighborhoods can be used to express the factual connection of a role to the specific term it specializes.

[32] Alternatively, these two properties may be shown instead in the associated annotation, thereby further reducing clutter. Reduce clutter wherever whenever you can!

[33] This categorization scheme can be based on some rule(s), but is not required to be.

[34] From ISO 704 [2000], "Terminology Work — Principles and Methods," p.9.

[35] This is a matter of some debate. For example, is it really useful to say *order consists of line items*?

[36] The double wavy line indicates that a meta level is being crossed.

[37] To avoid clutter, make ample use of neighborhoods to depict such instance-level terminology.

38 Only these 'lowest-level' things should be viewed as *individuals*; that is why this discussion uses *instances* throughout. Note also that since this discussion is about business vocabulary, I have assiduously avoided mentioning the common IT practice of using *type codes* to organize the associated data.

39 As before, I mean *technical* here in the sense of IT — not in terms of the products or services of the business. These products or services might, of course, be highly technical in their own right.

Chapter 5

A Closer Look at Rules

Rules apply to a broad spectrum of needs. To illustrate, consider the following situation that might occur in a baseball game. Suppose it is the bottom of the seventh inning, with two outs, two strikes on the batter, and two base runners. The score is tied. The batter is left-handed.

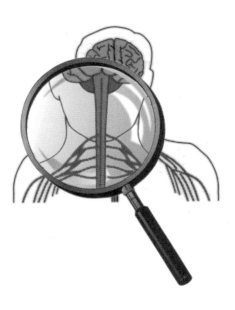

- A validation rule might ensure the batter still gets only three strikes even if the pitcher is changed.
- A computation rule might compute the batter's hit percentage in similar prior circumstances.
- Inference rules might help choose the best relief pitcher.

Rules cover all such needs, and more. They offer a unified approach to capturing, evaluating, and managing the spectrum of operational guidance.

Do rules fall into fundamental categories? Fortunately, *yes*. This chapter expands on the discussion in Chapter 2 to look at categorization of rules from two perspectives: first from the perspective of business people, then from the perspective of automated information/knowledge systems. Along the way, we will also look at exceptions to rules, clarifications and guidelines, decision tables, rule quality, and more.

To start off, however, let's take a closer look at the question: *What exactly is a business rule?*

What is a Business Rule?[1]

A *business rule* is simply a rule that is under business jurisdiction. *Under business jurisdiction* is taken to mean that the business can enact, revise, and discontinue their business rules as they see fit. If a rule is not under business jurisdiction in that sense, then it is not a business rule. For example, the 'law' of gravity is obviously not a business rule. Neither are the 'rules' of mathematics.

> A business rule is simply a rule
> that is under business jurisdiction.

The more fundamental question in defining *business rule* is the meaning of *rule*. Clearly, *rule* carries the sense of *guide for conduct or action* both in everyday life and in business. One way or another, this sense of *rule* can be found in most, if not all, authoritative dictionaries.

> Rules serve as guides for conduct or action.

Examining the matter more closely, if rules are to serve as guides for conduct or action, they must also provide the actual criteria for judging and guiding that conduct or action. In other words, for the context of business rules (and probably in most other contexts), rules serve as *criteria* for making decisions. A business definition of *rule* therefore encompasses the sense of *criteria* as given by authoritative dictionaries.

> Rules provide criteria for making decisions.

Business rules are just part of the larger issue of how guidance is created and delivered within business.[2] Figure 5–1 presents an overall categorization of guidance from the perspective of business people.[3] From that perspective, all rules are either *operative* or *structural*, as discussed in the subsections that follow. Use Figure 5–1 as a reference for the rest of this chapter.

Compared with a *business policy*, a rule needs to be *actionable*. This means that a person who knows about a rule could observe a relevant situation (including his or her own behavior) and decide directly whether or not the business was complying with the rule. In general, a *business policy* is not actionable in that sense; policy must be interpreted into some more concrete business rule(s) that satisfy its supposed intent. For example the following business policy is not actionable: *Safety is our first concern.* Note the fact type in Figure 5–1: *business rule is derived from business policy.*

> Rules must be actionable.

For a rule or other element of guidance (e.g., a clarification) to be actionable assumes that the business vocabulary on which it is based has been adequately developed, and has been made available as appropriate. Note the fact type in Figure 5–1: *element of guidance is based on fact type*. In the business rule approach, all elements of guidance are based on a structured business vocabulary. Rules and other elements of guidance are established on top of that vocabulary in building-block fashion. For more on that important idea, refer to Chapter 4, which presented numerous examples of rules.

Just because rules are actionable does *not* imply they are always automatable — many are *not*. For instance, consider the (actionable) rule: *A hard hat must be worn in a construction site.* Non-automatable rules need to be implemented as user activity, and supported by procedure manuals or rulebooks. In many ways, managing non-automatable rules is an even more urgent matter for the business than managing automatable ones.

> Non-automatable rules should be managed too.

Figure 5–1. Categorization of business guidance.

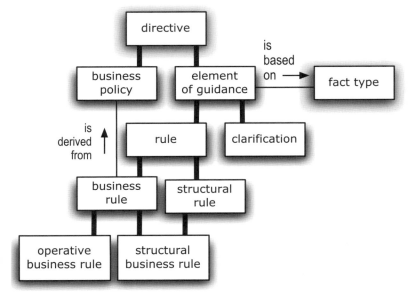

Operative Rules

Consider the business rule: *A gold customer must be allowed access to the warehouse.*[4] Clearly this rule can be violated. If a gold customer is denied access to the warehouse (assuming there are no extenuating circumstances, such as exception rules), then a violation has occurred. Presumably, there is some sanction(s) associated with such violation — for example, the security guard might be called on the carpet.

Any rule that can be violated *directly* by people involved in affairs of the business is an *operative rule*. Operative rules govern the on-going conduct of business activity, always carrying the sense of *obligation* or *prohibition*. To reflect that sense, *RuleSpeak* prescribes the rule keywords *must* or *only* to express operative rules.

> **A business rule that can be violated directly is an operative rule.**

One way or another, operative business rules are always preventative, as the following examples illustrate.

- *Surgical gloves must be worn in performing surgery.*
  This rule is intended to prevent infections.
- *A nurse must visit a patient at least every 2 hours.*
  This rule is intended to prevent inattention to patients.
- *A gold customer must be allowed access to the warehouse.*
  The rule is intended to prevent any denial of access.

Operative business rules enable the business to run (i.e., to *operate*) its activities in a manner deemed suitable, optimal, and/or best aligned with its goals. Operative rules deliberately preclude specific possibilities (of *operation*) that are deemed undesirable, less effective, or potentially harmful. Often, sanction is real and immediate if an operative rule is broken.

Operative rules are a distinctive feature of the business rule approach.[5] All operative rules are business rules.

As discussed in Chapter 6, operative rules have significant (and perhaps surprising) consequences for business processes — that is, for how work should be organized. A key question in that regard is how the business *selectively* responds to violations of particular rules (if at all!). This, in turn, raises the issue of how strictly each operative rule should be enforced — that is, its appropriate *level of enforcement*. There is much more to discuss in that regard, but let's save that for the next chapter.

Structural Rules

Additional rules would be relevant to evaluating the operative rule: *A gold customer must be allowed access to the warehouse.* Specifically, what criteria should be used for determining whether a particular customer is *gold* or not? Here is an example: *A customer is always considered a gold customer if the customer places more than 12 orders during a calendar year.*

Such rules are called *structural rules.*[6] Structural rules are about how the business organizes (i.e., *structures*) its basic knowledge, always carrying the sense of *necessity* or *impossibility*.[7] To reflect that sense, *RuleSpeak* prescribes the rule keywords *always* or *never* to express a structural rule.[8]

> Operative rules shape business conduct;
> structural rules shape business knowledge.

If a customer appears at the warehouse, but the security guard is unaware of the criteria expressed in the structural rule, or misapplies the criteria, quite possibly the customer will not be given due access. The error, however, manifests itself in the form of a violation of the operative rule, *not* the structural rule(s) per se. Structural rules can be ill-conceived, misunderstood, or misapplied, but they cannot be directly violated.

> A structural business rule can be ill-conceived, misunderstood,
> or misapplied, but it cannot be violated directly.

Structural business rules enable the business to create (i.e., to *structure*) its own private world of encoded knowledge. They give shape (i.e., *structure*) to core concepts of the business by precisely establishing clear lines of demarcation for each. They also allow the business to extrapolate its knowledge in a highly organized (*structured*) fashion via inference and computation rules (more on this later). During business activity, structural rules are used to evaluate 'where you are' (current state of affairs) as the need arises. For example:

- Is this customer a gold customer or not?
- Do we owe this customer a discount on this order?
- Does this patient have cat scratch fever or something else?

The conclusion reached in each case is only as good as the guidance within the rules. Poor or misapplied guidance yields poor or inconsistent results. In that case, some aspect of the encoded knowledge 'breaks down' — it simply does not work properly.

This is a fundamental difference between operative rules and structural rules. Disregard for operative rules leads to violations and possible sanctions; misapplication of structural rules leads to mistakes and undesirable results — but only indirectly, if at all, to violations.

Structural Rules and Definitions

Based on the discussion above, it would seem that structural rules, in contrast to operative rules, are more 'definitional' in nature. In a general sense, that is true. In practice, however, a clear distinction nonetheless can and should be maintained between definitions and structural rules.

As discussed in Chapter 4, a good definition focuses on the essence of a concept — the core meaning of the concept to the business. Structural rules, in contrast, indicate the exact lines of demarcation — that is, the precise 'edges' of the concept. In other words, structural rules provide definitive criteria to determine when something *is or is not an instance of a concept.*

> Structural rules provide criteria for when something is or is not an instance of a concept.

For example, consider an 'essence' definition of *gold customer:* a customer that does a significant amount of business over a sustained period of time. Now compare that with the associated structural rule: *A customer is always considered a gold customer if the customer places more than 12 orders during a calendar year.*

The definition provides the fundamental notion about what *gold customer* means to the business. It is unlikely that basic notion will change — in other words, the notion as defined in this manner is very stable. The structural rule, in contrast, gives specific criteria for determining whether a customer is or is not *gold* — criteria that quite possibly will change over time. As indicated in Chapter 4, any aspects of business practice subject to change should be treated as rules, not embedded in definitions.

Another difference between definitions and structural rules is that the latter frequently provide criteria that would not be so obvious from the definition, for example: *A customer is never considered a gold customer if the customer has been incorporated less than a year.*

Chapter 5

Inference and Computation Rules

Structural rules such as those above — although not in the form of *if-then* statements — actually represent inference rules.[9] A complex decision may involve hundreds of inference rules, or even more. Their evaluation, however — no matter how many rules are involved — cannot directly result in a violation. Although the result might be quite serious for the business — perhaps even calamitous — technically, no violation has occurred. The result would simply represent a really, really bad decision.

> **Inference rules can be misapplied or result in bad decisions, but cannot be violated per se.**

What about rules that express how to compute some mathematical result? Consider the following example: *The total price of an order item is always computed as the product unit price times its quantity.* This rule

prescribes criteria for exactly how the result, *total price of an order item,* is to be computed. The rule can be evaluated to actually produce that result. The prescribed criteria might, of course, be inadequate or mis-specified, but that simply represents poorly developed guidance, not any violation. Computation rules are therefore also structural rather than operative.

> **Computation rules provide criteria for how results are to be computed.**

What if someone attempts to calculate *total price of an order item* using some criteria other than that specified by the rule above. Wouldn't that be a violation?

If a rule has been specified for how to compute a named result, it must be assumed to 'win' over any other non-rule means to compute that given result. (Otherwise, why bother specifying the rule?!) So if some business worker(s) or IT developer(s) wish to calculate the result using other criteria, they can; they just need to name the result differently. For example, they might call their result *amount charged to customer for order item.* However, in that case the business would probably want an additional rule: *The <u>amount charged to a customer for an order item</u> must be equal to the <u>total price of that order item</u>.* This new rule clearly could be violated — it is therefore *operative.*

Suppose a salesman decides to give a special volume discount to a personal friend. Again, the original computation rule is merely for computing; it does not prohibit inappropriate conduct. For that, the business would need a separate (operative) rule — for example: *A special volume discount may be given only to high-volume customers.*

> Computation rules do not prohibit undesired conduct;
> they cannot be violated per se.

Rule Reduction

When rules are first captured, they often embed multiple criteria that need to be broken out as separate rules. Breaking them out is called *rule reduction.*[10] As discussed in Chapter 2, the goal is to produce highly-granular expressions of business guidance that can be independently re-used and modified.

A best practice in rule reduction is never mix criteria for how a computation should be performed in the same rule as do's and don'ts about applying the result. In other words, avoid intermingling structural and operative criteria in the same rule. Following this guideline not only enhances clarity with respect to both kinds of criteria, but also improves granularity.

> Avoid mixing operative and structural criteria in the same rule.

To quickly illustrate both rule reduction and the application of this principle, consider the following extension to the sample computation rule above: *The total price of an order item is always computed as the product unit price times its quantity minus 10% if the order is the first order ever placed by the customer.* Rule analysis could should result in the following, more granular rules.

Rule 1 (Structural): *The first-time discount is always computed as 10% times the total price of an order item.*

Comment: To reduce the complexity of rules, always break out computations as separate rules as soon as possible.

Rule 2 (Structural): *The first-time discount is always considered an applicable discount for each order item of the first order that a customer places.*

Comment: Be alert to any more general concept(s) not originally mentioned by the rule that might apply. For example, the first-time discount is perhaps just one of many discounts that sometimes might be *applicable* to order items.

Rule 3 (Structural): *The total price of an order item is always computed as the product unit price times its quantity, minus applicable discounts.*

Comment: This is the original computation rule; the generalized notion about subtracting applicable discounts has been appended.

Rule 4 (Operative): *The amount charged to customer for an order item must be equal to the total price of that order item.*

Comment: This is the operative rule given earlier; its expression has not been impacted by the new structural rules.

Exceptions

Consider the operative rule: *A library card must not be held by more than one borrower, unless one of the borrowers is Bill Gates.* This rule includes a clear-cut exception. The normal rule for library cards is: *A library card must not be held by more than one borrower.* Loosely stated, the exception

is: *Don't enforce this normal rule if Bill Gates is one of the borrowers for the library card.*

Don't enforce, of course, is not declarative. Instead, we should say something more *rule-ish* such as: *must not be enforced.* The exception now reads: *The normal rule for a library card must not be enforced if Bill Gates is one of the borrowers for the library card.* What emerges is another rule![11]

Unfortunately, the business rule approach offers no silver bullet to the *business* problem of having too many exceptions to rules (which many companies do!). However, by always viewing exceptions as simply more rules, exceptions are at least put onto the same playing field as other rules. For reengineering business processes and/or streamlining business operations, that positioning can sometimes represent an important breakthrough in and of itself.

> Exceptions to rules always represent more rules.

Clarifications and Guidelines

Consider the statement: *A bank account may be held by a person of any age.* Although the statement certainly seems to give business guidance, it does not directly:

- Place any obligation or prohibition on business conduct.[12] (Therefore it is not an operative rule.)
- Establish any necessity or impossibility for knowledge about business activities. (Therefore it is not a structural rule.)

In short, it is not a rule, but rather a *clarification.*[13]

Is it important then to write it down (i.e., capture and manage it)? *Maybe.* Suppose the statement reflects the final resolution of a long-standing debate within the business about how old a person must be to hold a bank account. Some say 21, others 18, some 12, and some say there should be no age restriction at all. Finally the issue is resolved in favor of no age restriction. It's definitely worth writing that down!

> Clarifications emphasize what is possible or permissible as a matter of current business policy.

Now consider the following statement: *An order $1,000 or less may be accepted on credit without a credit check.* This clarification is different. It suggests a rule that possibly hasn't been captured yet: *An order over $1,000 must not be accepted on credit without a credit check.* Assuming

the business wants this rule, you should write *the rule* down — not the clarification — because the rule provides more explicit guidance.[14]

Suppose this operative rule is restated as follows: *An order over $1,000 should not be accepted on credit without a credit check.* Note the *should* where before *must* was used. Now is it a clarification?

No. It is still a rule, only with a lighter sense of prohibition. What actually changed was its presumed *level of enforcement.* Rather than strictly enforced, now the rule has the sense: *It's a good thing to try to do this, but if you can't there's no sanction.*[15] In other words, now it's simply a *guideline* (or *suggestion,* if you prefer).

> A guideline is an operative rule with no tangible enforcement.

Should you use *should* or *should not* (or similar forms) to express lightly-enforced operative rules? *Not recommended* (in spite of the use in the example above). In general, it's better to use consistent wording for all operative rules (e.g., *must* or *must not*). Remember, the level of enforcement for any given rule often varies with changes in business practice. Guidance is one thing; level of enforcement is another — best not to mix the two! By the way, this is why you do not find *guideline* in Figure 5–1.

The really important thing is that guidelines, like clarifications and all other rules, use the same underlying vocabulary. Note that in Figure 5–1 *all* elements of guidance *are based on* fact types. Let's put it this way: If you have the vocabulary to express rules for behavior, you already have the vocabulary you need for guidelines and clarifications.

> Business rules cover all forms of actionable guidance.

Decision Tables

As you scale up, having an effective means to visualize and manage entire *sets* of rules at a time becomes more and more important. Decision tables are excellent in that regard. In general, decision tables can be used where these three criteria are met:

1. A significant number of rules are parallel — that is, they share the same subject, have exactly the same evaluation term(s), and are equivalent (but not identical) in effect. In other words, the rules all share a common pattern and purpose.

2. Each evaluation term has a finite number[16] of relevant instances.[17]

3. Given the different instances of the evaluation term(s), the outcomes cannot be predicted by a single formula. (If a single formula could predict the outcomes, using a single rule or set of rules to give the unified formula is a better approach.)

> **Decision tables represent sets of rules.**

Here is a simple example.

Rule 1: Applicable sales tax is to be 6.0% if year = 1999.
Rule 2: Applicable sales tax is to be 6.5% if year = 2000.
Rule 3: Applicable sales tax is to be 6.5% if year = 2001.
Rule 4: Applicable sales tax is to be 6.5% if year = 2002.
Rule 5: Applicable sales tax is to be 6.25% if year = 2003.[18]
Rule 6: Applicable sales tax is to be 7.0% if year = 2004.
Rule 7: Applicable sales tax is to be 8.0% if year = 2005.
Rule 8: Applicable sales tax is to be 8.15% if year = 2006.

Note that this set of rules satisfies all three criteria above:

1. The eight rules are exactly parallel. They share the same subject, applicable sales tax; have exactly the same evaluation term, year; and are equivalent (but not identical) in effect, an indicated sales tax percentage for each given year.

2. The evaluation term, year, has a finite number of relevant instances (eight).

3. The outcomes — the percentages indicated for applicable sales tax — cannot be predicted by a formula.

> Decision tables are an excellent means
> to visualize and manage parallel rules.

The following rule, along with Decision Table A, shows the consolidated business logic for the eight rules given above. I think you'll agree it's quite an improvement!

Rule: Applicable sales tax is to be the percent value in Decision Table A for a given year.

Decision Table A

Year	Applicable Sales Tax
1999	6.0
2000	6.5
2001	6.5
2002	6.5
2003	6.25
2004	7.0
2005	8.0
2006	8.15

Decision tables are also useful for finding missing rules — that is, for assessing the *completeness* of a rule set. For example, if any cell in a decision table has nothing in it, then that outcome is possibly missing and probably should be addressed.[19] I will return to the crucial issue of completeness a bit later.

Decision Table A has only a single evaluation term. Most decision tables have more than that. To illustrate, the following rule, along with Decision Table B, adds a second evaluation term *county* to determine *applicable sales tax*.

Rule: Applicable sales tax is to be the percentage in Decision Table B for a given year and county.

Decision Table B

County

Year	Harkin	Lopes	Qwan	Quail
1999	6.95	8.2	7.35	4.0
2000	6.73	8.3	9.0	4.5
2001	6.15	8.4	9.0	5.0
2002	6.15	8.3	9.0	5.5
2003	6.15	8.4	6.75	6.0
2004	6.15	8.2	6.75	6.75
2005	5.75	8.2	6.75	7.0
2006	5.95	8.4	7.5	7.25

Representing *more* than two evaluation terms using a two-dimensional media (for example, paper) is problematic.[20] If there are three or more evaluation terms, with all but two (or fewer) being simple,[21] the business logic can still be represented in variations of the two-dimensional format used thus far.[22] Beyond that, some different approach is required. The following rule, along with Decision Table C, illustrates.

Rule: The delivery method for an order is to be as in Decision Table C.

Decision Table C

Delivery Method for an Order

Decision Criteria	Picked Up by Customer	Shipped by Normal Service	Shipped by Premium Service
Rush order	No	Yes	Yes
Order includes fragile item	No	Yes	—
Order includes specialty item	No	No	—
Order includes high-priced item	No	No	—
Order includes item involving hazardous materials	No	Yes	Yes
Category of customer	Silver	Gold	Platinum
Destination of order	—	Local	Remote

Decision Table C establishes the basis for determining the delivery method for an order. Three possible delivery methods (the outcomes) are indicated along the top. Seven decision criteria[23] appear at the left as labels for the rows.[24] Six of these decision criteria are binary (*yes, no* or *local, remote*), whereas one, *category of customer*, involves three possibilities (*silver, gold, platinum*). The choice of delivery method for an order depends on what appears in the cells of a column. A dash (—) in a cell indicates that the associated decision criteria does not matter in determining the outcome; that is, *any* alternative for that decision criteria will produce the same outcome.

Unfortunately, such multi-dimension decision tables are prone to anomalies and other problems, so they must be developed with care and then scrutinized closely. For example, consider the issue of completeness. How complete is the sample decision table above? *Not very!* Can you tell why? The answer is worked out in a note at the end of the chapter.[25]

> Special analyses can be performed on decision tables
> to ensure rule quality.

Rule Quality

Determining the quality of large sets of rules — their *fitness* — is an issue of foremost concern not only to rule analysts, but to business people as well. Fortunately, Rule Independence[26] opens significant opportunities in this area. Never before has the business been in a position to shape and refine its own guidance and know-how so *directly* and *proactively*. Assessing the quality of rules falls into two general areas: *validation* and *verification*.

> Rule quality requires both validation and verification.

Validation means assessing fitness with respect to *business purpose*. The goal is not only to ensure correctness of the rules from the perspective of business people but also to ensure that, when applied, the results will be appropriate in all relevant circumstances. Validation is largely a matter of analysis, but there are many ways in which automated analysis tools can help. For example, diagrams can depict logical or computational dependencies between rules; test scenarios can be retained so prior results can be compared with new results for modified rule sets; rules can be analyzed to identify all events where they need to fire to ensure complete coverage; etc.

Verification means assessing fitness with respect to *logical consistency*. Verification is always performed on an entire rule set at a time, looking for two or more rules that in combination exhibit some anomaly. Below is a quick sampler of common anomalies, along with simple examples. Can you figure out what's going on in each case?

Linguistic Equivalences

* *A permanent employee must receive a salary.*
* *An employee who is permanent must receive a salary.*

Modal Equivalences

* *An order over $1,000 must not be accepted on credit without a credit check.*
* *An order over $1,000 may be accepted on credit only with a credit check.*

Logical Equivalences

* *A high-risk customer must not place a rush order.*
* *A rush order must not be placed by a high-risk customer.*

Subsumations

* *A rush order must have a destination.*
* *An order must have a destination.*

Conflicts

* *A shipment must include more than 1 order.*
* *An out-of-state shipment may include only 1 order.*

In practice, remember that rules are often captured by different people at different points in time, so such anomalies can appear even in the best-coordinated efforts. By the way, such anomalies are not the result of a rule-based approach; rather, they are just much easier to spot. Fortunately, comprehensive detection of such anomalies can be automated. There is only one caveat, but it's a big one: *You must coordinate the business vocabulary the rules use.*

> **Your automated work environment for managing business rules should provide analysis tools that directly address rule quality.**

An additional area of concern in rule quality, as mentioned for decision tables, is the *completeness* of rules — that is, whether there are gaps or holes in coverage. As a simple example, consider the clarification discussed earlier: *An order $1,000 or less may be accepted on credit without a* *credit check.* A missing rule might be: *An order over $1,000 must not be accepted on credit without a credit check.*

One final word: Rule quality is not an IT issue — it's primarily a business one. You want to ensure quality *before* rules are translated into an implementation language (so business people can better understand them)[27] and/or are used in production (so you don't have to detect anomalies *live*[28]). Doesn't that really go without saying?

> Rule quality tools should work on rules
> expressed from the perspective of business people, not IT.

Match Making

Some of the most complex business problems addressed by rules involve two or more sets of instances that must be matched in optimal fashion (*best fit*). Such *match-making* problems — also sometimes called *pattern matching* — are quite common in business processes and decision-making.

The business rule approach generally focuses on doing things as near to real-time as possible, so that errors and violations don't compound themselves downstream. However, matching instances of two or more sets in real time (i.e., one by one, as the instances become available) often does not produce the best fit. A *set-at-a-time* approach frequently does much better. Applied prudently, it need not risk any compliance problems. The following simple example illustrates.

Suppose that multiple items must be packed in optimal fashion into multiple boxes of a certain size. Every item has both a volume and a dollar value. *Optimal* in this case means the following:

• Try to pack all items into boxes.

• If that proves impossible (e.g., because there are not enough boxes, the items are too bulky, etc.), then pack only the items that will maximize the total dollar value packed in the boxes.

Six items arrive one at a time by conveyor belt. There are just three boxes. By coincidence, the first three items off the conveyor belt are very bulky, filling the three boxes completely. Unfortunately, these first three items are of considerably less total value than the next three items (which might happen to be quite small). Instance-at-a-time allocation does not produce the best packing results. A better approach is to wait until all six items have arrived via the conveyor belt (or as long as possible, anyway), and then perform the allocation on a *set-at-a-time* basis in order to achieve the best fit possible.

This box-packing example has two best-fit goals — *pack all items* vs. *maximize total packed item value*. Although some match-making problems have only a single goal, the more interesting (and complex) are multi-goal. At some level, multiple goals almost inevitably conflict.

> Match-making problems often involve conflicting goals.

Other examples of best-fit problems and the types of goals they entail include the following:

- Rental car allocation at an airport branch of a rental car agency.
  Satisfy all reservations and upgrade rules vs. *maximize profits.*

- Airline rebooking of all passengers on a cancelled flight.
  Select the best flights for customers vs. *minimize the company's financial loss.*

- Medical diagnosis.
  Match the most symptoms of the patient vs. *match the most discriminating ones.*

- Job assignments.
  Meet the individual preferences of each applicant vs. *satisfy the requirements of each position available.*

> Match-making problems are common in operational business processes and decision-making.

Generally speaking, optimization with respect to best-fit goals will be better the longer you wait to perform the match making. For example, in the box-packing example, waiting for all six items to come off the conveyor belt will often produce a better solution than waiting for fewer. However, business circumstances generally preclude waiting indefinitely. For example, suppose the items are perishable and can remain unpacked for no more than 30 minutes. This critical timing threshold can be expressed as a rule.[29]

To optimize any given match-making problem, someone in the organization (a *subject matter expert*) generally must have relevant knowledge and experience.[30] For example, the most experienced personnel in the shipping department may be able to describe the steps or decision sequence they follow in performing the optimization manually. Their step-by-step approach will include heuristics (e.g., *always pack the most valuable item first*) to be applied in some logical sequence.[31]

Any solution for a pattern-matching problem — best fit or otherwise — usually must comply with certain rules. An example for the box-packing case might be: *The volume of an item that can be packed in a box is always less than or equal to the volume of an available space within the box.*

Such rules are often numerous and complex, representing significant know-how of the business.

> Match-making problems often involve large numbers of rules representing significant business know-how.

Rules in Information/Knowledge Systems

So far in this chapter we have looked at rules only from the perspective of business people and rule analysts. Rules from the perspective of automated information/knowledge systems are obviously also of interest. The remainder of this chapter focuses on that.

Rules arise from two (and only two) sources for automated information/ knowledge systems: (1) Transformation and/or translation of *business* rules into implementation form, and (2) Creation of new rules pertaining strictly to system design itself. In this discussion, rules from both sources are called *system rules*.[32] System rules from the latter source have no *business rule* counterparts — a very important distinction! As discussed below, system rules come in three *functional categories*[33] — *rejectors, producers,* and *projectors*[34] — based directly on how they respond to *update events*.

As introduced in Chapter 2, an update event is something happening in an automated information/knowledge system that needs to be noted or recorded because knowing about the event is potentially important to other activities, either those occurring during the same time frame or those that might happen later. In other words, an update event occurs anytime the *state*

of the information/knowledge system changes. That *state* can be supported in various ways (for example, as a database design, a class diagram, and so on). To simplify matters, let's just say there is some data somewhere in the system that must be updated (created, modified, or deleted) to record each event.

Rejectors

Many system rules are naturally *rejectors* — that is, left to their own devices,[35] they simply reject any event that would cause a violation to occur.[36] The specific sequence of activity might be:

1. An end user initiates a procedure to do some work, for example: *Take a customer order.*

2. The end user's activity produces an update event to record the results of the work, for example: *Create an instance of order.*

3. The update event causes a system rule to fire,[37] for example: *An order must have a ship-to address.*

4. The system rule checks whether the end user has actually given a ship-to address with the order. Suppose the end user has not done so.

5. The system rule causes the update event to be rejected — that is, the action fails, and the order is not created.[38]

In their basic form, rejectors are narrow-minded. Either the end user plays by the rules, or the work will not be accepted. If there is any question about the quality of the work — that is, about the correctness[39] of data that would result from it — the work will simply be rejected. In other words, rejectors *insist* upon data quality and do so by active, real-time interventions in ongoing work.[40] Because rejectors emphasize real-time enforcement — that is*, real-time compliance* — they play a high-profile role in the business rule approach.

> Rejectors address data quality
> by supporting real-time compliance.

So far, a strict level of enforcement for rejectors has been assumed. Does it always have to be strict? *No.* Can it be simply suggested? *Yes.* What happens in that case?

For one thing, the rejector loses its bite — so let's call it a *suggestor*.[41] Also, recall from Chapter 2 that (in general) every rule always needs to be evaluated for two or more relevant kinds of update events. The firing of a suggestor occurs just as for any other rule. Specifically, it fires upon the occurrence of any of the two or more kinds of update events where it could be 'violated.' Normally a rejector would reject any update event that would cause a violation. As a suggestor, no such enforcement action is taken.

Instead, the end user is simply informed. As always, the rule statement should pop up on the end user's screen (if authorized). Rather than conveying an error, however, it informs the worker that under the given circumstance some particular action (update event) is, or is not, appropriate. In short, suggestors impart business knowledge in real time, but exercise no control.

> Suggestors impart knowledge in real time to influence, but not control, how work is conducted.

Producers

A *producer* never rejects update events. Instead, it always just accepts them and automatically computes (or derives) something. In performing this computation the producer uses all relevant data, whether old or new (i.e., the new current state). For example, in taking an order, a producer might re-compute the current order total each time a new line item for the order is entered.

Producers automate computations. In other words, no extra programming is required to implement them. The results computed from a producer are guaranteed both current and correct.[42] Moreover,  since producers (like all rules) are generally multi-event, rule-based computation means there is no chance of missing less-than-obvious kinds of events where re-computation is needed.

Producers are really simply *functions* defined in *rule-ish* manner. Producers seem much friendlier than rejectors because they do not inhibit update events but rather provide additional mileage from them. Their overall purpose is to boost end-user (and/or programming) productivity.

> Rule-ish functions enhance productivity.

Projectors

A *projector* is the exact opposite of a rejector in a fundamental way. Specifically, a projector never rejects update events. Instead, it always accepts any relevant event and, as a response,[43] automatically takes some additional action — that is, *projects* that event into some other kind(s) of update event. There are many kinds of automatic update events that projectors can cause, but among the most important are:

- Inference: Infer appropriate conclusions from new (and existing) knowledge (i.e., new current state), providing automated assistance in making decisions.
- Triggers: Execute processes and procedures automatically.

Like producers, projectors work to provide additional mileage to update events, providing automatic value-adding behavior. In doing so, they eliminate that behavior as a user responsibility.

> Projectors provide automatic value-adding behavior.

Logic Traces

The results from evaluating (i.e., *reasoning over*) large numbers of inference rules in an automated information/knowledge system can sometimes prove unexpected or non-intuitive. Often, the end-user or rule analyst will want to ascertain *how* the results were produced — that is, audit them — preferably in real time. This means starting with the results and tracing back through the chain of rules that fired.

Such *logic traces* are an important capability for rule or inference engines to provide. A trace permits flaws and/or opportunities for improvement in decision logic to be identified. It also provides a means for less knowledgeable workers to learn about business *know-how* in hands-on fashion. Business guidance in production should always be *visible* to authorized users.

> Decision logic used in production
> should be visible to authorized users.

Summary

Rule Independence is the centerpiece of the business rule approach. The various principles underlying Rule Independence are enumerated in the *Business Rules Manifesto*,[44] a copy of which can be found at the end of this book.

One consequence of Rule Independence is that business rules become an object of study and expertise in their own right — a new and exciting business competency. This chapter has outlined the fundamentals of that competency with strong focus on the perspective of business people.

There is still more to come. Looking ahead to Chapter 6, one result of Rule Independence is a dramatic simplification of processes. To borrow a popular IT buzzword, taking out the rules means processes become *thin*. *Read on!*

Notes

---

[1] Much of this subsection is drawn from SBVR [2005]. For background on the SBVR and the consortium that produced it, refer to Editors of BRCommunity.com [2005].

[2] Sometimes called, or considered part of, the *governance process.*

[3] Also from SBVR [2005]. The diagram is given using FACT notation. Refer to Chapter 4 for explanation.

[4] Since this discussion is informal, I will again (as in Chapter 2) use the word *rule* instead of the more correct *rule statement* to refer to expressions of rules. The distinction is that the same rule can be given by statements in different forms and/or by statements in different languages (for example, French, Mandarin, and so on). In other words, there can be many different *rule statements* for exactly the same *rule.* The same holds true for clarifications, and indeed, for any element of guidance.

[5] Because operative rules can be broken, they require special treatment by formal logic. For example, consider the operative rule: *A gold customer must be allowed access to the warehouse.* It cannot be assumed that the rule has always been faithfully enforced; therefore, it cannot be inferred that in every situation where it was appropriate for a gold customer to be allowed access to the warehouse, the customer actually *was* allowed such access. In other words, certain kinds of *reasoning* must be carefully restricted for operative rules.

[6] Operative vs. structural rules is a distinction introduced by SBVR [2005],

[7] Unlike operative rules, not all structural rules are business rules. The reason is that not all structural rules are under business jurisdiction. As mentioned, the 'law' of gravity is obviously not under business jurisdiction. Neither are the 'rules' of mathematics. This distinction is the cause of the more complicated categorizations in Figure 5–1 pertaining to *structural* elements of guidance.

[8] All examples of structural rules in this discussion use these keywords (or permissible variations) for clarity and emphasis. For practitioners new to expressing rules, however, distinguishing between operative vs. structural rules via selective keywords should not be considered the matter of greatest concern. For that reason, the convention was not used in Chapter 2.

[9] The *if-then* form for the last rule, for example, is: *If a customer has been incorporated less than a year, then the customer is not a gold customer.* RuleSpeak disfavors the *if-then* form for numerous reasons. For one thing, it is unnatural for expressing most operative rules. For structural business rules, the business need is generally focused more on defining the precise 'edges' of business concepts — definitional matters — rather

than on extrapolating knowledge (i.e., if we know *this*, then we can know *that* for sure). That's not to say automated inferencing (reasoning based on inference rules), as in rule or inference engines, is not useful — *it most certainly is!*

10 During rule capture, the most important goal is simply to capture as full an understanding of the rule as possible. *Reduction* can be done later.

11 Exception rules represent the way people actually communicate — not the way rules might be handled in formal logic or by some rule or inference engines *under the covers*. Indeed at some level, exceptions may disappear altogether, their conditions being included in other rules. It would be very nice if the resulting forms remained business-friendly, but that seldom happens. As discussed in Chapter 3, experience demonstrates that managing rules for business people is simply a different problem than rendering rules for suitable treatment by rule or inference engines.

12 *Indirectly*, it does. The reason any guidance is written down (captured and managed) is presumably because the business wants workers and other parties to abide by it. If a worker refuses to give a person a bank account because of age, such action runs counter to the explicit guidance. However, it would be impractical to have a rule for every clarification simply instructing workers to abide by it.

13 'Affirmation' or 'admonishment' might be more precise.

14 Just because the clarification says *an order $1,000 or less may be accepted on credit without a credit check*, that does not necessarily mean an order over $1,000 *must not*. The rule, in contrast, can be presumed to indicate *over $1,000* explicitly because the obligation to do a credit check does *not* apply below that threshold.

15 Remember that only operative rules have level of enforcement; structural rules can't be violated.

16 To address a class of things that has an unlimited set of instances, the word *other* is sometimes used to represent all instances not specifically enumerated.

17 Or collections of instances, usually represented as ranges of values (a.k.a. *brackets*).

18 Note that the sales tax rate decreased in 2003 from the previous year. This decrease represents an apparently infrequent (and perhaps improbable!) tax cut.

19 If a majority of cells have nothing in them, a decision table might not be the best way to represent the given set of rules.

20 At this point an automated support tool becomes indispensable.

21 An example of *simple* would be *is order overdue?* which can be answered by only *yes* or *no*.

[22] For example, using (a) split rows and/or columns within a single array, or (b) multiple arrays, with one array per relevant instance or bracket of one (or more) of the evaluation terms.

[23] Since some are (simple) logical expressions, *decision criteria* is more appropriate here than *evaluation terms*.

[24] This table therefore involves seven dimensions.

[25] The completeness of the sample decision table can be calculated as follows:

(1) The total number of *possible* combinations for the instances of the seven decision criteria can be calculated as: $2^6 \times 3 = 192$. This calculation reflects the fact that six of the decision criteria apparently have two alternatives each (*yes* and *no* for five of them, and *local* and *remote* for the other), whereas the seventh (category of customer) apparently has three (*silver*, *gold*, and *platinum*).

(2) The total number of combinations *actually represented* in the table can be determined as follows. Column 2 represents one combination — each cell has something in it. Columns 1 and 3 are a bit more complicated because they both have one or more cells with dashes, indicating acceptance of any alternative — for example, either *yes* or *no*. Column 1 includes one such cell, so that column actually provides the basis for establishing the outcome for *two* combinations — one if the cell had had *local* and one if it had had *remote*. Column 3 includes three such cells, so that column actually establishes the basis for 2^3 or 8 outcomes. Altogether, the decision table actually establishes the basis for establishing 11 outcomes ($2 + 1 + 8 = 11$).

(3) Having determined how many combinations the decision table actually addresses (11), we can now determine how many it does not: $192 - 11 = 181$. *So some 181 possible combinations have not been addressed at all!* We must therefore conclude this decision table is *not very complete.*

[26] Refer to the BRG's *Business Rules Manifesto* presented at the end of this book for a complete look at Rule Independence.

[27] A major goal of SBVR [2005] is to enable specification of rules in such a way that no translation into any additional implementation language(s) is required.

[28] Or not. More worrisome in many respects are the anomalies you never find out about.

[29] This temporal rule might actually initiate the match-making and any additional tasks (workflow).

[30] Fortunately, match-making specifications need not always be developed from scratch. Instead, a more generalized solution for the basic pattern,

called a *framework,* might be available that can be specialized for the problem at hand. For example, there are all kinds of things in the world that need to be packed, loaded, bundled, or stored — not just items-into-boxes.

31 A rule engine or inference engine cannot implement rule-based optimization unless these heuristics — *rules* — are captured and encoded.

32 As discussed in Chapter 3, a crucial element in rule management is traceability of business rules to/from system rules.

33 Refer to Chapter 10 of Ross [2003] for a more complete discussion of the three functional categories.

34 Operative business rules that are automatable are generally translated into rejectors; structural business rules are generally translated into either producers or projectors.

35 Often, such system rules are not left entirely *to their own devices.* For example, when a rejector fires and a violation is detected, a user-friendly system might automatically offer a procedure or script that the end user can follow to correct things. Such capability is discussed in Chapter 6.

36 Rejectors are constraints, but then, in formal logic, so are projectors. Using the term *constraint* exclusively for rejectors can therefore be misleading, even though a common practice in IT.

37 As mentioned in Chapter 2, *fire* in this discussion means loosely both *execute* — to evaluate the relevant condition(s) — and, if necessary, invoke appropriate action. In some rule technologies, *fire* is used to refer only to the latter.

38 As before, I'm ignoring an obvious opportunity here to invoke an appropriate procedure or script to allow the end user to correct the violation immediately.

39 Technically, the correct word is *consistent.* Ensuring *correctness* from a business perspective is beyond the capability of rules or machines.

40 Specifically, a rejector can prevent the results of a processing action from being recorded if the rejector is not satisfied with them.

41 From Ross, Ronald G. [1997].

42 That is, *correct* given how the rule was specified. If the rule was specified imprecisely, the results might not be as intended.

43 Projectors have sometimes been called *stimulus/response* rules.

44 Business Rules Group [2003].

Chapter 6

A Closer Look at Work and Processes

What do business rules have to do with work[1]? That's no idle question. After all, it's doing the work that gets the product out the door and into the customers' hands. Your business faces a host of challenges in that regard, including:

Time shock: As the rate of change accelerates, workers are constantly thrust into new roles and responsibilities. They must be guided through unfamiliar procedures and/or business know-how as thoroughly and as efficiently as possible. The business pays a price, either directly or indirectly, if getting the workers up to speed is too slow (or too painful). *Time shock* is like culture shock — very disorienting if you're not prepared for rapid immersion.

> Time shock is like culture shock — very disorienting if you're not prepared for rapid immersion.

Training: The flip side of time shock is training — *how* to get workers up to speed. Training is expensive and time-consuming. Yet as the rate of change accelerates, more and more (re)training is required. Where do you turn for solutions?

> Keeping workers up to speed must be part of every process.

Adaptability: In the National Football League (NFL), if a play is not working for a team, it will be gone from its playbook in short order (possibly along with a coach or two). New plays can be deployed rapidly. In effect, the plays are essentially *throwaways* — cheap enough to discard readily, with minimum disruption or cost. Businesses urgently need something similar — throwaway procedures cheap enough to replace readily when they no longer work well (make 'yardage') for the business.

> **Businesses need throwaway procedures cheap enough to replace readily.**

The reason NFL plays can be treated as throwaways is that the knowledge necessary to run them is embodied elsewhere — in the scoreboard,[2] in the skills of the players, in the heads of the coaches, and most importantly, in the NFL rulebook. *A real-world example of Rule Independence!*

Another important direction for many companies today is managing business activity on more of a beginning-to-end, value-add basis. That requires thinking cross-organizationally about fundamental business processes. Are *throwaway* procedures compatible with managing business activity on a *process* basis? Can you have the best of *both* worlds?

Yes. Here's the short answer why. When business people talk about fundamental business processes they (quite naturally) mean *process* from a business perspective. Value chains simply don't change that fast. With throwaway procedures, *process* is viewed from the perspective of system design. Processes involved with automated information/knowledge systems *do* need to change rapidly. And they *can*!

> **Businesses can manage by business process and have throwaway procedures.**

The long answer why will take a bit more discussion, so let's get into it. First I will examine the relation of processes and rules from the perspective of business people, then later from the perspective of system design. In both cases, I think you'll come to agree with me: there's something really powerful afoot here!

Chapter 6

How Rules Relate to Business Processes

The best definition of *business process* I have seen is:[3]

Business process: *the tasks required for an enterprise to satisfy a planned response to a business event from beginning to end with a focus on the roles of actors, rather than the actors' day-to-day job*[4]

What do rules do for business processes? Roger Burlton says it this way: "If you separate the rules, you can develop remarkably stable processes."[5] If you are looking to manage business activities on a process basis that's exactly what you need. He goes on to say: "The really rapid change is in the rules ... <u>not</u> in the business processes." *Yes!*

> The really rapid change is in the rules,
> not the business processes.

How do rules and business processes interact? Burlton observes that business processes "... transform inputs into outputs *according to guidance* — policies, standards, rules, etc...." The key phrase in that is *according to guidance*. Exactly what does it mean? In some ways the answer is straightforward, but in others it is more subtle — and even more potent.

Structural Rules and Business Processes

Chapter 5 examined two categories of rules: structural rules and operative rules. Let's start with structural rules, whose relation to *business process* is a direct one. They simply off-load work pertaining to knowledge. There are at least two ways in which this happens:

Computation. Computation rules provide the business logic to perform any calculations that can be encoded. Such computation logic can be highly complex, involving many rules.

Decision Making. Inference rules can determine the proper outcomes at decision points ('branch points') in a business process. Such decision-making rules can range from simple (e.g., *has this product been discontinued* or *is this a repeat customer*), to quite complex (e.g., *is this insurance claim potentially fraudulent* or *what is the best of available job position for this applicant*). Complex cases can involve large numbers of inference rules. All such logic can be off-loaded from the business process.[6]

> Structural rules off-load work pertaining to knowledge
> from business processes.

Operative Rules and Business Processes

Now let's look at how operative rules relate to *business process*. As explained in Chapter 5, operative rules are ones that *people* can *violate*. In a game of football, operative rules are why you need referees on the field during each game — someone to watch and intervene if any violations occur. Operative rules, which arise anytime *people* are involved (not just knowledge), are a distinctive feature of the business rule approach.

> Operative rules arise anytime
> people are involved (not just knowledge).

Operative rules monitor on-going work as it occurs in the business process. The particular aspect of work they monitor ranges from specific to quite general:[7]

Iteration. Business processes often involve iteration (loops). Timing and repetition criteria for these loops can be expressed as rules. Examples include:

Maximum time allowed between iterations.

For example: *Additional information must be requested at least every 5 days if appropriate information is not received.*

Minimum time allowed between iterations.

For example: *Additional information must not be requested more often than every 24 hours.*

Maximum iterations permitted.

For example: *The total number of requests made for additional information for a claim must not exceed 10.*

Maximum time permitted for completion.

For example: *Requests for additional information for a claim must not be made after 10 days.*

Service Level Agreements. A service level agreement generally involves four things: (1) an action item, (2) a party, (3) escalation criteria, and (4) timing criteria. For example: *A customer service request must be brought to the attention of a supervisor if the request is not resolved within 4 hours.* In other words: (1) the action item *customer service request* (2) must be brought to the attention of a *supervisor* (3) if *not resolved* (4) *within 4 hours.*[8]

Compliance. A business process can involve hundreds of rules (or more!) addressing specific things *people* need to do to comply with business policy and/or external regulation. A business process cannot possibly address that many rules directly, especially if it's developed with a goal of managing business activity on a cross-organizational basis.[9] What do you do about that? Do what comes naturally — maintain a separate *rulebook*, as in football. The business process can focus on *a planned response to a business event from beginning to end*; the rulebook can focus on the guidance the business process needs to follow.[10]

> Operative rules off-load work pertaining to compliance
> from business processes.

Best Practices in Designing Business Processes with Rules

Structural rules tell you what you *should* or *could* do; what people *actually* do is another matter. Having flesh-and-blood people involved 'in the loop' for knowledge-rich business processes makes a big difference. Best practices in designing business processes with rules *and people* include:

1. *Avoid mixing structural and operative criteria in the same rule.*[11]
   Do people 'in the loop' need to abide by specific computed or inferred results of structural rules? If so, specify an operative rule. For example, inference rules may indicate whether or not an applicant for insurance satisfies all prerequisites. Operative rules indicate whether the decision-maker(s) in the loop *must* accept a qualified applicant and/or must *not* accept an *unqualified* applicant.

> Operative rules should indicate
> whether people must abide by computed or inferred results.

2. *Create separate tasks for creation of special knowledge and for people to take business action.*
   The knowledge tasks (e.g., determining the suitability of an applicant) can be based on structural rules[12]; the take-action tasks (e.g., hiring the applicant) can be monitored by operative rules.

> Work to create special knowledge should be
> separated from work to take business action.

3. *Consider the cost of rules in developing the business process.*
In business terms, it would be *very* costly (if even possible) to gather *all* the data that *any* structural rule in a business process might need. For example, a car insurance company might have the rule: *An applicant for car insurance is never considered qualified if the applicant is less than the minimum driving age.* Other rules might involve creditworthiness (which could involve an extensive credit check), previous driving history (which could require requesting records from the state), and so on. If it can be determined right off the applicant isn't old enough, that's obviously something you want to do. So a basic goal in designing business processes with rules and people is *work avoidance* (no pun intended) — test the cheapest rules first wherever possible. That just makes good business sense!

> **Avoid unnecessary work in a business process
> by designing it to test cheap rules first wherever possible.**

4. *Separate planned responses to violations of a rule from the rule itself.*
The appropriate response to violations of some rule can be given by: (a) some other rule(s) and/or (b) some process(es). These other rule(s) generally prescribe the appropriate sanction(s); the process(es) generally prescribe the appropriate means of detection/reaction.[13] Consider the *offside* rule in the game of football: *A player must not be offside.*[14] Associated with this rule are both:

a. A rule prescribing the appropriate sanction: The offside team in a play must be penalized five yards.

b. A planned means of detection/reaction:[15] The line judge watches, blows a whistle, throws a flag, stops the play, etc.

You should explore these two aspects for each operative rule guiding the business process.

> **Plan responses to violations of rules
> as more rules and/or processes.**

Chapter 6

Business Processes vs. System Processes

Rules relate to both business processes and system processes. In each case, rules serve to guide the processes. Having looked now at rules and processes from the perspective of business people, what about rules and processes from the perspective of information/knowledge system design?

Let's stand back and look for a moment at the 'big picture' concerning models in general. How does *any* model of the business (including its processes) differ from *any* model for the design of a system (including processes)?

John Zachman[16] describes the crucial difference this way. A business model "... is about real-world things." A system model, in contrast "... involves *surrogates* for the real-world things so that the real-world things can be managed *on a scale and at a distance that is not possible in the real world*. These surrogates are the things making up ... systems" [emphasis added].The most obvious kind of *surrogate for real world things* is data.[17] A system process includes actions that manipulate data in various ways, to:

- Request it. For example: *Obtain credit rating for a customer from the credit system.*
- Store it.[18] For example: *Store customer information.*
- Modify it. For example: *Modify year-to-date claimant payments.*
- Display it. For example: *Display customer's current account balance.*
- Communicate it. For example: *Insert a special order into a supervisor's work queue for approval.*

> System processes manipulate surrogates
> standing in for real world things.

A *system process* can manipulate other kinds of surrogates as well, for example:

- The supervisor's work queue is actually a *surrogate* for a face-to-face interaction between a supervisor and an order clerk each time a special order is received.

- The supervisor's GUI for displaying orders in the queue is actually a *surrogate* for the flesh-and-blood order clerk.

A system process then is all about manipulating surrogates standing in for real-world things. A *business process*, in contrast, should never include tasks or steps for manipulating surrogates. That's a *big* difference because the designs for how processes manipulate the surrogates is something you want to be able to change — often quite rapidly. *Like football plays!*

> Designs for how processes manipulate surrogates
> are what you want to be able to change rapidly.

Scripts — Thin Processes

When the rules are taken out of a system process, the result is a *thin process.*[19] *Thin* means that the process prescribes *only* the necessary series of steps to accomplish the desired work result. Excluded are all the rules — and all the error handling when violations of rules occur.

> Externalizing rules produces thin processes.

A football play is a good analogy. A diagram of a football play is literally represented as a collection of orchestrated steps needed to accomplish the desired result (advance the ball). It is nothing more and nothing less. No

rules — or penalties for violating these rules — are embedded within it. A play simply focuses on *doing the work.*

For an information/knowledge system, the 'plays' are the system processes, which we call *scripts.*[20] Scripts provide patterns for manipulating surrogates — that is, for doing work from the perspective of a system design. Scripts might be used to take a customer order, evaluate a medical claim, book a reservation, assign a teacher to a class, and so on. Often a script is undertaken in response to something that somebody does (for example, a customer placing an order). A script can also be undertaken in response to some timing criteria (e.g., when to bill customers), or to some predefined condition (e.g., inventory quantity on hand is below a certain threshold).[21]

> Scripts provide patterns for doing work
> from the perspective of system design.

Series of steps is an apt description of a script; *prescribed series of requests* is even better.[22] By *requests* I mean requests for action, which can be of various kinds — the very same kinds mentioned earlier. These requests are generally handled by software components presumed to execute. Such software components might include DBMSs,[23] GUIs, service providers (e.g., print routines), interfaces to legacy systems, work queues, special-purpose rule analyzers, and so on.

> A script is a thin process consisting of
> a prescribed series of requests.

Including People in Scripts

In many respects, the most important sources or recipients of requests in scripts are people. People, after all, do a lot of actual work! These people[24] might be either *inside* the company (that is, workers) or *outside* the company (e.g., customers). Although all these people might be seen as 'users', we like *actor* better.[25]

> Scripts involve people too.

What can human actors do to move work along? Two things: (a) perform actions — manually or otherwise — and (b) make requests for action to software components or to other actors.

Here then is the beginning of a new image for work:
- Many kinds of human and software actors interacting under scripts.
- Thin, throwaway scripts featuring choreographed collaboration.
- And rules!

> Scripts prescribe throwaway collaborations
> involving both people and machines.

Smart Scripts

As mentioned earlier, a foremost cause of *time shock* for business people is rapid change in the rules. At any given time, actors participating in scripts might be found at virtually any stage of time shock. Sometimes, you might find them completely up-to-speed, other times completely lost. Most of

the time, they are probably somewhere in between. That poses a big challenge with respect to *training*.

The only approach to training that will truly scale is on-the-job *self*-training. That requires *smart* scripts, ones coordinated with rules so that *pinpoint guidance* can be put right in front of actors in real time as the need arises[26] — that is, right at the *points of knowledge*.[27]

> The only approach to training that will scale
> is on-the-job self-training, right at the points of knowledge

Where do you find these points of knowledge? Two places:

* Wherever a human actor might not understand or might disagree with the results from structural rules.[28]
* Wherever a human actor could violate an operative rule.[29]

This second one has especially powerful implications for all rules that are automatable. What guidance message should be returned to an actor when such a rule is violated? As discussed in Chapter 2, *the guidance message should succinctly state the business rule that was violated.* What that means, in effect, is that the relevant portion[30] of the rulebook is 'read' to the actor on-line, right as the actor bumps up against the rule. Remember, the really rapid change is in the rules — these days, *no* worker can safely assume immunity from time shock.

> Business rule systems are instructional —
> form-fitted knowledge companions.

Rule-Based Process Re-Usability

Scripts imply reuse of software as a given.
Over and above that, scripts offer *process*
reusability. With rules, that means a lot more
than simply 'modular design'. [31]

Rule-based re-use of processes is distinctive
of the business rule approach. It works like
this. A script for undertaking work in normal
circumstances is invoked as the designated
response to the violation of some rule. [32] That
script kicks off automatically whenever a
violation of the rule is detected. [33]

> Rule-based re-use of processes is distinctive
> of the business rule approach.

Table 6–1 shows what such activity would look, like step-by-step, using
this simple scenario to illustrate:

Work script: *Take customer order.*

Rule: *A customer who places an order over $1,000 must hold an
account.*

Should the rule be violated in this script, invoke the script: *Establish
customer account.* [34]

Table 6–1. Step-By-Step Activity for Rule-Based Re-Use of a Process

	Step-by-step Activity	Simple Scenario
1.	A worker executes a script	A worker (order entry clerk) performs a script (*Take customer order*) to take an order.
2.	The worker makes a request under that script.	The worker (order entry clerk) makes a request (that the order be stored).
3.	The request produces a change in state.	Change in state (storage of the order) is attempted.
4.	The event results in the evaluation of relevant rules, if any.	This event fires the rule: *A customer who places an order over $1000 must hold an account.*
5.	A violation of one of these rules, let's suppose, is detected.	Let's say the customer holds no account, so a violation of the rule is detected.
6.	Another script (designated beforehand by the rule analyst or process analyst) is invoked automatically.	The script *Establish customer account* had been designated beforehand as the one to be invoked for a violation of this rule.
7.	This other script offers the capability needed for the original worker (or possibly someone else) to correct the error that caused the violation.[35]	The order entry clerk is offered the opportunity to perform the script *Establish customer account.*
8.	Supposing such work is undertaken under the offered script (not a given) ...	The order entry clerk elects to do so.
9.	And supposing such work is deemed satisfactory by the rule ...	This work successfully corrects the original violation of the rule — the customer now holds an account.
10.	Then work can continue under the *original* script from where it left off.	The order entry clerk resumes work under the original script, *Take customer order*, from the point it was interrupted. For example, the next action might be to schedule the order's fulfillment.

Chapter 6

Adaptability and Granularity

In closing this discussion of processes in automated information/knowledge systems, let's take one last hard look at *adaptability*. A general principle for software engineering is: The more *granular* the specifications for a system, the more *adaptable* it will be. Rule-related specifications for business rule systems are *highly* granular in these ways:

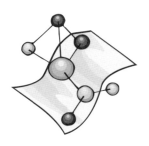

- *Separation of events and rules*, as enabled by declarative expression of rules. Refer to Chapters 2 and 5 for additional discussion.

- *Separation of rules and processes*, as prescribed by Rule Independence. The benefits accrue for both rules and scripts. A rule can be revised, replaced or eliminated without touching any script(s) at all.

- *Separation of scripts and violation responses for rules*, also supported by scripts. Specifically:

  1. A script designated for violations of a rule can be revised, replaced, or eliminated *without touching* the rule itself or any script that might produce violations of it.

  2. Any script that might produce violations of a rule can be revised, replaced, or eliminated *without touching* the rule itself or the script designated for handling violations of the rule.

- *Level of enforcement* for rules, which provides an entirely new area of granularity. Possible levels of enforcement[36] are presented at the end of this chapter, which also identifies some of the implications for script design.[37] The possibilities are exciting and powerful!

> Business rule systems are highly adaptable for business needs because their rule-related specifications are highly granular.

Summary

The business rule approach offers powerful innovations for processes. By taking the rules out, processes are greatly simplified. In addition:

- From the business perspective, the separation of rules and processes also yields stable processes that can serve as a framework for managing business activity.

- From the system perspective, the separation of rules and processes also yields thin processes that are highly adaptable.

Rule Independence changes the very nature of work. Take a quick look at the Business Rules Manifesto (following the end of this chapter) if you haven't done so already. To put it as simply as possible, business rules are about working *smarter*.

Business rules are about working smarter.

Chapter 6

Notes

¹ I don't mean anything special by *work* in this chapter. Here is the relevant MWUD definition: 1: activity in which one exerts strength or faculties to do or perform; 1a: sustained physical or mental effort valued as it overcomes obstacles and achieves an objective or result

² The names of the variable information posted on the scoreboard are terms that represent some of the most basic concepts of the game of football — for example, *quarter, time, score, down,* etc.

³ At time of this writing, I am not aware of any standard industry definition for *business process.*

⁴ Janey Conkey Frazier (Swimlane Process Maps), actually given for *workflow.*

⁵ Roger Burlton, Process Renewal Group, a noted authority on business process.

⁶ This does *not* have to happen all at once. In other words, you do *not* have to know and encode all the rules in advance. For example, a decision point may be handled manually at first, and only later be automated using encoded inference rules, as time, cost, and feasibility permit. Business rule systems are quite good at supporting *continuous improvement* methodologies.

⁷ We might add *dependencies* to the list, for example: *A claimant may be notified that a claim has been denied only if the claim has been adjudicated.* I haven't done so because simple dependency rules like this can be embedded in the process notation. Whether you should embed them that way or specify them independently is a matter of preference and pragmatics.

⁸ Actually, this rule could be broken into three more atomic rules through *rule reduction*:

(1) *A customer service request must be resolved in timely fashion.*

(2) *A customer service request not resolved in timely fashion must be brought to the attention of a supervisor.*

(3) *In timely fashion is to be 4 hours.*

Rule 2 expresses the appropriate business response to a violation of rule 1. In general, such responses are always specified by some rule(s) and/or by some process(es). As a best practice, an operative rule should always be expressed independently of any response to a violation so rule and response can change independently. (*Granularity* always helps achieve adaptability.) Rule 3 avoids embedding ('hard coding') the same timing criteria, *4 hours,* into the other two rules. (Extracting and *localizing* such criteria also helps achieve adaptability.)

⁹ Actually, that would be even more difficult than it would seem at first

glance. As discussed in Chapter 2, most rules involve *two or more* events where they need to be evaluated. Consider the rule: *A customer must be assigned to an agent if the customer has placed an order.* This rule involves two events: (1) *When* a customer places an order (an obvious one), and (2) *When* an agent leaves the company (a less obvious one). A business process that focuses on fulfillment of customer orders is very unlikely to address the second event.

[10] As discussed in Chapter 3, this rulebook should be automated using a knowledge-smart work environment for managing business rules at the business level, which should also support interrelations with the processes.

[11] This best practice was introduced in Chapter 5, which provided additional discussion and examples.

[12] Usually inference rules, rather than computation rules, unless the computation is complex.

[13] For convenience, I have ignored several important things here, both discussed later.

- Level of enforcement. Often, rules for public consumption are not the real rules — that is, the ones actually enforced. For example the posted speed limit on a highway might be 55 mph. The real rule, meaning the one strictly enforced (if detected), might be 63 mph.

- Whether the rule is automatable. If an operative rule can be automated, detection of violations is removed as a business concern. In addition, if you simply want to prevent violations — not invoke sanctions or anything else — reaction to violations (in the form of preventing update events) are also removed as a business concern. That assumes, of course, the system can prevent any event that causes the violation (generally not the case for motorists speeding!).

[14] For the sake of convenience, I have also ignored structural rules to determine *offside.*

[15] The planned reaction might be an entire business process in its own right, but generally it is not. Instead, it is often assigned as a job responsibility (e.g., for the line judge), especially if not automatable.

[16] Refer to Zachman, John A. [2002].

[17] That's why a data model and a fact model are fundamentally different. A fact model is how we talk about *real-world things* using a structured business vocabulary. A data model is how we organize *surrogates* for the real-world things in the form of data.

[18] In a file or database.

[19] Only a relatively small portion of traditional application code literally supports the actual steps of a system process. Much of the code is devoted to edits, validations, derivations, and calculations — in other words, to rules — as well as to the associated detection/reaction responsibility.

²⁰ By 'we' I mean Business Rule Solutions, LLC in its business rule methodology, *Proteus™*. Using *script* rather than *system process* emphasizes: (a) the critical shift in perspective needed in moving from a *business* perspective to a *system* perspective, and (b) a re-orientation to rule-friendly process design.

²¹ In both these cases, appropriate criteria for automatically initiating the scripts can be expressed as rules.

²² *Prescribed* means that the given series of steps *can* be followed to achieve the desired results, but not that they *must* be followed. For example, there might be one or more other series of steps that can be followed to achieve the same results. To say *must be followed* represents a rule about sequencing, or more precisely, about *required antecedents*. It is a matter of preference and pragmatics whether that kind of rule should be embedded in the notation for system processes, graphic or otherwise. In Proteus-style scripts, we prefer not to; as a result, any series of requests is merely *prescribed* (not mandatory).

²³ To create, retrieve, modify, or delete data.

²⁴ We need to be careful here in keeping our perspectives straight. To allow for connecting to people *on a scale and at a distance that is not possible in the real world,* it's not actually the *real* person — it's a surrogate via a logical communication link.

²⁵ The term *user* suggests outside beneficiaries of system services, whose own work and interactions are outside scope. *Actor*, in contrast, suggests someone whose own activity or role is integral to understanding and doing the work. An actor is someone whose own work is definitely *within* scope.

²⁶ Assuming the given actor is authorized.

²⁷ Refer to Chapter 3.

²⁸ As discussed in Chapter 5, these will be *producers* and *projectors* from the perspective of system design.

²⁹ As discussed in Chapter 5, these will be *rejectors* from the perspective of system design.

³⁰ *Relevant portion* probably means structural rules as well.

³¹ This form of re-use occurs when one script uses (requests) some other script to do a step of its own work. Since the second script is not embedded within the first, the second can be requested (re-used) by *other* scripts as well. For example, the script *Fill out address* could be potentially (re)used by the scripts: *Take customer order, Record prospect information, Create shipment, Hire employee,* and so on. This kind of reuse, which involves no special use of rules, is commonplace (and quite important) in building business systems.

[32] Invocation can be for all scripts, a given script, or a particular point in a script, and optionally for only a given class of actor or individual actor. Invocation can also be subject to rules — for example, timeframe criteria.

[33] This invocation capability, as well as the capability to detect violations, is assumed to be an automatic (built-in) part of the system. Support by a rule engine or similar platform is clearly desirable. In any case, support should never be part of any script (or other portion of an application) but, rather, provided by software infrastructure.

[34] Let's say this is the script normally used to set up accounts, so there's a good chance it would be already familiar to the order entry clerk.

[35] This is typical, but not the only kind of reaction possible. A script invoked for a security breach, for example, might focus on immediate countermeasures.

[36] Adapted from SBVR [2005].

[37] Possible levels of enforcement for rules are presented in Table 6-2 (opposite), which also identifies some of the implications for script design. Not included in this list is 'not tested' — that is, not even evaluated, much less enforced or suggested. The rule with this level of enforcement might literally be just for show (public consumption). More likely, the rule is not being tested because it is pending or retired; deemed inapplicable or overly expensive; etc. Obviously there are no direct implications for designing scripts in such a case. If the violation is time-based, the event generally cannot be prevented.

Chapter 6

Table 6–2. Levels of Enforcement for Rules and Their Implications for Designing Scripts

Level of Enforcement	Description	Implication for Designing Scripts
strictly enforced	If an actor violates the rule, the actor cannot escape sanction(s).	When a violation is detected, the event producing the violation is automatically prevented, if possible,[+] and a designated violation response, if any, is invoked automatically.
deferred enforcement	The rule is strictly enforced, but such enforcement may be delayed — e.g., until another actor with required skills and/or proper authorization can become involved.	When a violation is detected, the event producing the violation is allowed, and the relevant work is handed off to another worker (possibly by insertion into a work queue). Additional timing rules may be desirable to ensure that action is taken in a timely fashion.
override by pre-authorized actor	The rule is enforced, but an actor with proper before-the-fact authorization may override it.	When a violation is detected, if the actor involved is pre-authorized, that actor is given an opportunity to override the rule. Overrides by actor and rule should be tracked for subsequent review.
override with real-time waiver	The rule is enforced, but an actor may request a real-time waiver from another actor having before-the-fact authorization to give such waivers.	When a violation is detected, the actor involved is given an opportunity to interactively request a waiver from a duly-authorized actor. Additional timing rules are probably appropriate. Waivers should be tracked by actor and rule for subsequent review.
post-justified override	The rule may be overridden by an actor who is not explicitly authorized; however, if the override is subsequently deemed inappropriate, the actor may be subject to sanction(s).	When an override of a violation occurs, a review item (with all relevant details) should be inserted into the work queue of an appropriate actor for review and possible action.
override with explanation	The rule may be overridden simply by providing an explanation.	When a violation is detected, the actor involved is given an opportunity to override the rule by providing a mandatory explanation. Overrides should be tracked by actor and rule for subsequent review.
guideline	Suggested, but not enforced.	When a violation is detected, the actor involved (if authorized) is simply informed/reminded of the rule.

Business Rules Manifesto[1]
The Principles of Rule Independence
by Business Rules Group

Article 1. Primary Requirements, Not Secondary
1.1 Rules are a first-class citizen of the requirements world.
1.2 Rules are essential for, and a discrete part of, business models and technology models.

Article 2. Separate From Processes, Not Contained In Them
2.1 Rules are explicit constraints on behavior and/or provide support to behavior.
2.2 Rules are not process and not procedure. They should not be contained in either of these.
2.3 Rules apply *across* processes and procedures. There should be one cohesive body of rules, enforced consistently across all relevant areas of business activity.

Article 3. Deliberate Knowledge, Not A By-Product
3.1 Rules build on facts, and facts build on concepts as expressed by terms.
3.2 Terms express business concepts; facts make assertions about these concepts; rules constrain and support these facts.
3.3 Rules must be explicit. No rule is ever assumed about any concept or fact.
3.4 Rules are basic to what the business knows about itself — that is, to basic business knowledge.
3.5 Rules need to be nurtured, protected, and managed.

Article 4. Declarative, Not Procedural
4.1 Rules should be expressed declaratively in natural-language sentences for the business audience.
4.2 If something cannot be expressed, then it is not a rule.
4.3 A set of statements is declarative only if the set has no implicit sequencing.
4.4 Any statements of rules that require constructs other than terms and facts imply assumptions about a system implementation.
4.5 A rule is distinct from any enforcement defined for it. A rule and its enforcement are separate concerns.
4.6 Rules should be defined independently of responsibility for the *who, where, when,* or *how* of their enforcement.
4.7 Exceptions to rules are expressed by other rules.

Article 5. Well-Formed Expression, Not Ad Hoc
5.1 Business rules should be expressed in such a way that they can be validated for correctness by business people.
5.2 Business rules should be expressed in such a way that they can be verified against each other for consistency.

5.3   Formal logics, such as predicate logic, are fundamental to well-formed expression of rules in business terms, as well as to the technologies that implement business rules.

Article 6. Rule-Based Architecture, Not Indirect Implementation

6.1   A business rules application is intentionally built to accommodate continuous change in business rules. The platform on which the application runs should support such continuous change.

6.2   Executing rules directly — for example in a rules engine — is a better implementation strategy than transcribing the rules into some procedural form.

6.3   A business rule system must always be able to explain the reasoning by which it arrives at conclusions or takes action.

6.4   Rules are based on truth values. How a rule's truth value is determined or maintained is hidden from users.

6.5   The relationship between events and rules is generally many-to-many.

Article 7. Rule-Guided Processes, Not Exception-Based Programming

7.1   Rules define the boundary between acceptable and unacceptable business activity.

7.2   Rules often require special or selective handling of detected violations. Such rule violation activity is activity like any other activity.

7.3   To ensure maximum consistency and reusability, the handling of unacceptable business activity should be separable from the handling of acceptable business activity.

Article 8. For the Sake of the Business, Not Technology

8.1   Rules are about business practice and guidance; therefore, rules are motivated by business goals and objectives and are shaped by various influences.

8.2   Rules always cost the business something.

8.3   The cost of rule enforcement must be balanced against business risks, and against business opportunities that might otherwise be lost.

8.4   'More rules' is not better. Usually fewer 'good rules' is better.

8.5   An effective system can be based on a small number of rules. Additional, more discriminating rules can be subsequently added, so that over time the system becomes smarter.

Article 9. Of, By, and For Business People, Not IT People

9.1   Rules should arise from knowledgeable business people.

9.2   Business people should have tools available to help them formulate, validate, and manage rules.

9.3   Business people should have tools available to help them verify business rules against each other for consistency.

Article 10. Managing Business Logic, Not Hardware/Software Platforms

10.1   Business rules are a vital business asset.

10.2   In the long run, rules are more important to the business than hardware/software platforms.

10.3   Business rules should be organized and stored in such a way that they can be readily redeployed to new hardware/software platforms.

10.4   Rules, and the ability to change them effectively, are fundamental to improving business adaptability.

Glossary[1]

Reference Sources	
[MWUD]	*Merriam-Webster Unabridged Dictionary* (Version 2.5). [2000]. Merriam-Webster Inc.
[SBVR]	The Business Rules Team. [April 2005]. *Semantics of Business Vocabulary and Business Rules (SBVR)*.

associative fact type: *a fact type involving two or more things in a manner meaningful to, and shaped completely by, the business*

assortment: *a factual connection template indicating that some thing is an instance of a class of things*

binary fact type: *a fact type that involves exactly two things*

business: [MWUD 'enterprise'] 1c: *a unit of economic organization or activity (as a factory, a farm, a mine); especially: a business organization : FIRM, COMPANY :* 1d: *any systematic purposeful activity or type of activity*

business capacity: *some significant subset of a business, possibly encompassing one or more business processes, functional areas, and/or decision points*

business event: *something that happens requiring the business to respond, usually in a non-trivial way and often following some pattern of activity developed in advance, for example, as a business process model, workflow model, procedure, etc.*

business rule: [SBVR] *a rule that is under business jurisdiction*

categorization: *a factual connection template indicating that some class of things is a category of some other class of things*

categorization scheme: *a scheme used to create two or more categories for a class of things (e.g., 'gender' is the scheme for categorizing people as 'male' and 'female')*

category: *a class of things whose meaning is more restrictive, but otherwise compliant with, some other class of things (e.g., person and organization are categories of party)*

clarification: [SBVR] *an element of guidance that something is permissible or possible, that there is no rule against it*

---

[1] I am calling this list of terms *glossary* rather than *Concepts Catalog* because it does not constitute a proper *structured business vocabulary*. Compare the three definitions to see why.

composition: *see* **whole–part**

concept: [MWUD] *something conceived in the mind* : *THOUGHT, IDEA, NOTION*: as b(1) : *an idea comprehending the essential attributes of a class or logical species* : c : *an idea that includes all that is characteristically associated with or suggested by a term* : *CONCEPTION*

Concepts Catalog: *a listing of the contents of a structured business vocabulary*

definition: [MWUD] 2: *a word or phrase expressing the essential nature of a person or thing or class of persons or of things* : *an answer to the question "what is x?" or "what is an x?"*

directive: [SBVR] *a means that defines or constrains some aspect of an enterprise*

elementary fact type: [SBVR] *a fact type whose facts cannot be split into smaller units of information that collectively provide the same information as the original*

enterprise: *see* **business**

fact model: *a visualization or blueprint of a structured business vocabulary*

fact type: *something specific that can be known about one or more thing(s) important to the operational business (e.g., that a customer can place an order)*

factual connection template: *a basic standard form of fact type having some predefined (built-in) meaning about how two or more things are related (e.g., that one thing can be a property of another thing)*

factual sentence form: *a wording for a fact type (e.g., customer places order)*

glossary: *a collection of terms limited to a special area of knowledge or usage*

governing rule: *any law, act, statute, regulation, contract, business policy, legal determination, etc. from which business rules can be interpreted*

guidance message: *a rule statement given at a point of knowledge*

n-ary fact type: *a fact type that involves more than two things*

Glossary

objectify: [MWUD] 1a: *to cause to become or to assume the character of an object² (e.g., the fact type* 'student enrolls in course offering' *could be objectified as* 'enrollment')

operative rule: [SBVR] *a business rule that there is an obligation concerning conduct, action, practice or procedure*

partitive: *see* **whole–part**

POK: *see* **point of knowledge**

point of knowledge: *any event in which guidance and/or the company's specialized know-how (a.k.a., business rules) is developed, applied, assessed, or retired*

property[1]: [MWUD] 1a: *a quality or trait belonging to a person or thing* d(1): *an attribute, characteristic, or distinguishing mark common to all members of a class or species*

property[2]: *a factual connection template indicating that something has a property*

reify: *see* **objectify**

role: *a point of involvement of something in a fact type*

rule: [MWUD 'rule'] 1a: *guide for conduct or action* 1f: *one of a set of usually official regulations by which an activity (as a sport) is governed [e.g.,]* *the infield fly rule* *the rules of professional basketball* [MWUD 'criteria'] 2: *a standard on which a decision or judgment may be based*

Rule Independence: *the externalization, unification, and management of rules separately from processes*

structural rule: [SBVR] *a rule that is intended as a definitional criterion*

structured business vocabulary: *the set of terms and their definitions, and all fact types, that organize the operational knowledge of a business capacity and/or its know how*

term: [MWUD] 8a: *a word or expression that has a precisely-limited meaning in some uses or is peculiar to a science, art, profession, trade, or special subject*

unary fact type: *a fact type that involves exactly one thing*

---

² The sense of *object* here is [MUWD] 1: *something that is put or may be regarded as put in the way of some of the senses : a discrete visible or tangible thing [for example:]* "saw an object in the distance"

update event: *an action taken in an information/knowledge system to indicate a change of state (in available knowledge about the business)*

whole–part: *a factual connection template indicating that some class of things (the whole) is composed of (typically) two or more other classes of things (the parts)*

References

Burlton, Roger T. [2001]. *Business Process Management: Profiting from Success.* Indianapolis, IN: Sams Publishing.

The Business Rules Group. [February 2005]. *The Business Motivation Model ~ Business Governance in a Volatile World* (Release 1.1). Available at http://www.BusinessRulesGroup.org formerly known as *Organizing Business Plans: The Standard Model for Business Rule Motivation*, (2000).

The Business Rules Group. [January 8, 2003]. *Business Rules Manifesto ~ The Principles of Rule Independence* (Ver. 1.2). Available at http://www.BusinessRulesGroup.org (in English as well as translations to other languages).

The Business Rules Group. [July 2000]. *Defining Business Rules ~ What Are They Really?* (4th ed). Available at http://www.BusinessRulesGroup.org formerly known as the *GUIDE Business Rules Project Report*, (1995).

The Business Rules Team. [April 2005]. *Semantics of Business Vocabulary and Business Rules (SBVR)*. Available at http://www.omg.org as bei/05-03-01: BRT's revised submission to the Business Semantics of Business Rules RFP.

Date, C. J. [2000]. *An Introduction to Database Systems* (7th ed.). Boston, MA: Addison-Wesley.

Editors of BRCommunity.com. [January 2005]. "A Brief History of the Business Rule Approach," *Business Rules Journal*, Vol. 6, No. 1. Available at http://www.BRCommunity.com/a2005/b216.html

Halpin, Terry. [2001]. *Information Modeling and Relational Databases: From Analysis to Logical Design.* San Francisco, CA: Morgan Kaufmann Publishers.

ISO 1087-1. [2000]. *Terminology Work — Vocabulary, Part 1: Theory and Application.*

ISO 704. [2000], *Terminology Work — Principles and Methods.*

Lam. Gladys S. W. [May/June 1998]. "Business Knowledge — Packaged in a Policy Charter," *DataToKnowledge Newsletter*, Vol. 26, No. 3. Available at http://www.BRCommunity.com/a1998/a385.html

Merriam-Webster Unabridged Dictionary (Version 2.5). [2000]. Merriam-Webster Inc.

Ross, Ronald G. [1997]. *The Business Rule Book* (2nd ed.). Houston, TX: Business Rule Solutions, LLC. Available at http://www.BRSolutions.com

Ross, Ronald G. [2003]. *Principles of the Business Rule Approach.* Boston, MA: Addison-Wesley.

Seer, Kristen. [May/July/Sept. 2002]. "How to Develop Effective Business Analysts" (Parts 1, 2, and Part 3), *Business Rules Journal.* Available at http://www.BRCommunity.com/a2002/b106a.html

Zachman, John A. [2002]. *The Zachman Framework: A Primer for Enterprise Engineering and Manufacturing* (electronic book). Available at http://www.zachmaninternational.com

Index